# ORGANIZATIONAL OVERSIGHT: PLANNING AND SCHEDULING FOR EFFECTIVENESS

David A. Erlandson
Peggy L. Stark
Sharon M. Ward

EYE ON EDUCATION
Suite 106
6 Depot Way West
Larchmont, NY 10538
(914) 833–0551
(914) 833–0761 fax

**Library of Congress Cataloging-in-Publication Data**

Erlandson, David A.
       Organizational oversight : planning and scheduling for
    effectiveness / David Erlandson, Peggy L. Stark,  Sharon M. Ward.
            p.    cm.
    Includes bibliographical references
    ISBN 1-883001-26-9
    1. School management and organization—United States.
2. Educational planning—United States.  3. Scheduling (Management)
—United States.  4. School principals—United States.   I.  Stark,
Peggy L., 1949-   .  II. Ward, Sharon M.,  1938-   .  III.  Title.
LB2805.E75     1996
371.2—dc20                                                        96-15147
                                                                      CIP

10 9 8 7 6 5 4 3 2

Editorial and production services provided by Richard H. Adin Freelance
   Editorial Services, 9 Orchard Drive, Gardiner, NY 12525 (914-883-5884)

## Published by Eye On Education:

**Block Scheduling: A Catalyst for Change in High Schools**
by Robert Lynn Canady and Michael D. Rettig

**Teaching in the Block**
edited by Robert Lynn Canady and Michael D. Rettig

**Educational Technology: Best Practices from America's Schools**
by William C. Bozeman and Donna J. Baumbach

**The Educator's Brief Guide to Computers in the Schools**
by Eugene F. Provenzo, Jr.

**Handbook of Educational Terms and Applications**
by Arthur K. Ellis and Jeffrey T. Fouts

**Research on Educational Innovations**
by Arthur K. Ellis and Jeffrey T. Fouts

**Research on School Restructuring**
by Arthur K. Ellis and Jeffrey T. Fouts

**Hands-on Leadership Tools for Principals**
by Ray Calabrese, Gary Short, and Sally Zepeda

**The Principal's Edge**
by Jack McCall

**The Administrator's Guide to School-Community Relations**
by George E. Pawlas

**Leadership: A Relevant and Realistic Role for Principals**
by Gary M. Crow, L. Joseph Matthews, and Lloyd E. McCleary

**Organizational Oversight:**
**Planning and Scheduling for Effectiveness**
by David A. Erlandson, Peggy L. Stark, and Sharon M. Ward

**Motivating Others: Creating the Conditions**
by David P. Thompson

**Oral and Nonverbal Expression**
by Ivan Muse

**The School Portfolio:**
**A Comprehensive Framework for School Improvement**
by Victoria L. Bernhardt

**School-to-Work**
by Arnold H. Packer and Marion W. Pines

**Innovations in Parent and Family Involvement**
by William Rioux and Nancy Berla

**The Performance Assessment Handbook
Volume 1: Portfolios and Socratic Seminars**
by Bil Johnson

**The Performance Assessment Handbook
Volume 2: Performances and Exhibitions**
by Bil Johnson

**Bringing the NCTM Standards to Life**
by Lisa B. Owen and Charles E. Lamb

**Mathematics the Write Way**
by Marilyn S. Neil

**Transforming Education Through Total Quality
Management: A Practitioner's Guide**
by Franklin P. Schargel

**Quality and Education: Critical Linkages**
by Betty L. McCormick

**The Educator's Guide to Implementing Outcomes**
by William J. Smith

**Schools for All Learners: Beyond the Bell Curve**
by Renfro C. Manning

# FOREWORD

The School Leadership Library was designed to show practicing and aspiring principals what they should know and be able to do to be effective leaders of their schools. The books in this series were written to answer the question, "How can we improve our schools by improving the effectiveness of our principals?"

Success in the principalship, like in other professions, requires mastery of a knowledge and skills base. One of the goals of the National Policy Board for Educational Administration (sponsored by NAESP, NASSP, AASA, ASCD, NCPEA, UCEA, and other professional organizations) was to define and organize that knowledge and skill base. The result of our efforts was the development of a set of 21 "domains," building blocks representing the core understandings and capabilities required of successful principals.

The 21 domains of knowledge and skills are organized under four broad areas: Functional, Programmatic, Interpersonal, and Contextual. They are as follows:

*FUNCTIONAL DOMAINS*
  Leadership
  Information Collection
  Problem Analysis
  Judgment
  Organizational Oversight
  Implementation
  Delegation

*PROGRAMMATIC DOMAINS*
  Instruction and the Learning
    Environment
  Curriculum Design
  Student Guidance and Development
  Staff Development
  Measurement and Evaluation
  Resource Allocation

*INTERPERSONAL DOMAINS*
  Motivating Others
  Interpersonal Sensitivity
  Oral and Nonverbal Expression
  Written Expression

*CONTEXTUAL DOMAINS*
  Philosophical and Cultural
    Values
  Legal and Regulatory Applications
  Policy and Political Influences
  Public Relations

These domains are not discrete, separate entities. Rather, they evolved only for the purpose of providing manageable descriptions of essential content and practice so as to better understand the entire complex role of the principalship. Because human behavior comes in "bunches" rather than neat packages, they are also overlapping pieces of a complex puzzle. Consider the domains as converging streams of behavior that spill over one another's banks but that all contribute to the total reservoir of knowledge and skills required of today's principals.

The School Leadership Library was established by General Editors David Erlandson and Al Wilson to provide a broad examination of the content and skills in all of the domains. The authors of each volume in this series offer concrete and realistic illustrations and examples, along with reflective exercises. You will find their work to be of exceptional merit, illustrating with insight the depth and interconnectedness of the domains. This series provides the fullest, most contemporary, and most useful information available for the preparation and professional development of principals.

> Scott D. Thomson
> Executive Secretary
> National Policy Board for
> Educational Administration

If you would like information about how to become a member of the **School Leadership Library**, please contact:

Eye On Education
Suite 106
6 Depot Way West
Larchmont, NY 10538
(914) 833–0551 Phone
(914) 833–0761 FAX

# ABOUT THE AUTHORS

David A. Erlandson, professor of Educational Administration at Texas A&M University, has written or edited several books and monographs related to the professional development of principals and has contributed numerous journal articles on the same or related topics. He received the Bachelor of Arts degree from Wheaton College, the Master of Science degree from Northern Illinois University, and the Doctor of Education degree from the University of Illinois. Prior to coming to Texas A&M University he served as a public school teacher and administrator in Illinois and as a professor in the school administration program at Queens College of the City University of New York.

Peggy L. Stark, principal of Sidney Lanier High in San Antonio, Texas, has also served as an elementary school teacher, an elementary principal, and a central office administrator. She received the Bachelor of Science degree from Olivet Nazarene University, the Master of Education degree from Trinity University, and the Doctor of Education degree from Texas A&M University. She has had extensive experience in various aspects of staff development and has provided in-service training to numerous groups of principals. In addition, she has made many presentations to professional audiences and has served as a consultant to various university research and development projects.

Sharon M. Ward, principal of Jasper Middle School, has spent her career as a teacher, a special educator, and an administrator in middle schools and high schools in Texas. She received the Bachelor of Education degree from the University of Houston and the Master of Education degree from Sam Houston State University. In addition to her present position as principal in Jasper, Texas, she has served as associate principal at McCullough High School in Conroe, Texas, and as an assistant high school principal in Bryan, Texas. Her wide experience and training have been frequently used in providing training to secondary school teachers and administrators.

# PREFACE

When one considers the complexity of the principal's job, it is truly amazing that there are principals who are effective in performing it. A look at the 21 domains that identify the knowledge and skills required for effective performance in the principalship documents the problem dramatically. Some observers, upon reviewing the domains, have declared the principal's job an impossible one and have called for a new school organizational structure that will not make such diverse and intense demands on one individual.

However, while different organizational structures have been proposed for providing leadership in the schools (e.g., teacher committees), none have demonstrated success over time or in the variety of school situations over which principals must preside. Research and other informed observations have consistently shown that effective principals are key figures in effective schools. But to escape from what might appear to be a tautology, we need to answer the question: "What makes an effective principal?"

David Erlandson, Peggy Stark, and Sharon Ward take the position that one critical factor in the application of the knowledge and skill base described by the 21 domains lies in the principal's ability to plan and to organize resources of time, personnel, and space to fulfill these plans for the school day, the school week, the school year, and the school's future. In short, they believe that the domain of Organizational Oversight is crucial if the other knowledge and skills possessed by the principal are to impact the schools. But effective organizational oversight cannot be accomplished by a principal sitting at his or her desk, out of touch with the school's stakeholders. Organizational oversight requires a foundation of mutual trust and fertile communication, the source and channel of effective planning.

Planning and organizing are not the sole province of the principal; the principal's success as a planner and organizer will depend to a great extent upon the degree to which he or she can make other stakeholders true partners in the process. Using many illustrations, the authors take time to describe a strategy for enhancing organizational trust and productive communication and to demonstrate how these can be used to plan and organize, both in maintaining the school organization and in adapting it for change.

This book is written for both current principals and for the professional educator who aspires to that position. Practical illustrations are used to enable the reader to make links with real life situations. Practical exercises for building one's organizational oversight skills are provided throughout the book. Timeless principles of human organization are developed in current terms and using current examples. This is a book that principals can profitably reread many times as their careers develop, learning new applications of these timeless principles as their own experiences expand.

David A. Erlandson
Alfred P. Wilson

# ACKNOWLEDGMENTS

The authors especially want to thank the many principals, assistant principals, and teachers who contributed their thoughts and experiences to the development of this book and who took the time to read through the manuscript and make recommendations for improving it.

# TABLE OF CONTENTS

# 1

# THE SCOPE OF ORGANIZATIONAL OVERSIGHT

This book addresses the domain of Organizational Oversight, one of the 21 domains of knowledge and skill deemed necessary for the principalship by the National Policy Board for Educational Administration (Thomson, 1993). The Board classified these domains into four groups: functional domains, programmatic domains, interpersonal domains, and contextual domains. These groupings divide the domains as follows:

*FUNCTIONAL DOMAINS*
- Leadership
- Information Collection
- Problem Analysis
- Judgment
- Organizational Oversight
- Implementation
- Delegation

*PROGRAMMATIC DOMAINS*
- Instruction and the Learning Environment
- Curriculum Design
- Student Guidance and Development
- Staff Development
- Measurement and Evaluation
- Resource Allocation

*INTERPERSONAL DOMAINS*
- Motivating Others
- Interpersonal Sensitivity
- Oral and Nonverbal Expression
- Written Expression

*CONTEXTUAL DOMAINS*
- Philosophical and Cultural Values
- Legal and Regulatory Applications
- Policy and Political Influences
- Public Relations

These 21 domains are not discrete from each other, but rather represent a convenient classification system for better examining, understanding, and enhancing the principalship. It would be hard, for example, to talk significantly about any of the functional or interpersonal domains without talking about leadership, yet each of these domains addresses aspects of the principalship that do not fall adequately under the single rubric of "leadership." Furthermore, the functional domain of leadership focuses on elements that can be distinguished from other domains. While there is blending between what Thomson describes as "converging streams of behavior" (1993, p. xiii), each domain makes a distinctive contribution to the principal's job. This book focuses on the contributions of the organizational oversight domain.

Organizational oversight schedules and coordinates the implementation of the other domains. It has a direct impact on all the others. For example, organizational oversight recognizes when "problem analysis" (another functional domain) will be required and what resources need to be allocated to it. Organizational oversight lets a principal know when "information collection" is needed, how and when "curriculum" must be developed and evaluated, when "written expression" should occur (e.g., scheduling the production of written reports), and when a leader must use "legal principles."

## A DEFINITION OF ORGANIZATIONAL OVERSIGHT

Let us examine now the National Policy Board's definition of organizational oversight:

> Planning and scheduling one's own and others' work so that resources are used appropriately, and short- and long-term priorities and goals are met; scheduling flows of activities; establishing procedures to regulate activities; monitoring projects to meet deadlines; empowering the process in appropriate places. (Thomson, 1993, p. 5-3.)

We shall systematically develop this definition throughout the book.

While the basic requirements for organizational oversight may be similar for all principals, factors such as the size and level of the school, the personnel and other resources that are available to it, and the nature and intensity of societal pressures will differ. Principals must work early in their tenure at schools to get a clear understanding of both the internal organization of the school and its external environment. They must assess carefully how to use and strengthen the resources they can control in order to move the school on a path that enhances the goals of education in a democratic society. Throughout the book we will illustrate our major themes with specific examples, knowing from the beginning that every school is different and will require different applications. Our illustrations are not intended as blueprints for what a particular school should do but as clarification of basic principles that can be adapted to any school.

Chapter 2 describes how a principal can enlist human resources to plan successfully. Through the maximization of valid information and through maximizing human involvement in the design and management of the school's tasks, the principal can empower the processes that drive daily school activity. All individuals in schools—teachers, students, and parents—should receive rewards for productive engagement in the planning and implementation of a school's operation. A healthy school exhibits a structure that offers such rewards, facilitates a flow of valid information, and fosters effective teamwork.

A vibrant and continually renewed vision provides the foundation for both long- and short-range planning. Chapter 3 describes how to institute and maintain a strategic planning process for the school. Strategic planning, which is a multiyear process, also provides a framework for mid-range planning—the organization of the school year. In Chapter 4, we describe some of the major tools that the principal may use to organize the school year: the master calendar, the master schedule, and the annual campus plan. Also discussed are ways to use standard documents, such as handbooks and brochures, to reach the school's various audiences. The same principles that help the principal organize the school year can also guide the daily activity and work flow of the school. Some tips for accomplishing this are presented in Chapter 5.

Planning implies intervening to bring about change, either to prevent some undesirable things or to produce a desirable result. Chapter 6 examines the complexity of implementing and monitoring the change process and provides practical advice to the principal for effecting change in the school.

The final chapter proposes and describes an organizational audit. Through this tool, the principal can assess the health of the school operation and consider ways to reorganize and renew.

## ORGANIZATIONAL OVERSIGHT AND PROGRAM EVALUATION

Although program evaluation is not the major focus of this volume (see the book in this series on Domain 12, Measurement and Evaluation), it is an integral part of planning, and planning is at the heart of organizational oversight. Some preliminary remarks will show how and why it relates to this book and what questions it leads principals to ask as they plan and guide the course of their schools.

Program evaluation is essentially an assessment by stakeholders using the following questions about the school organization:

- What should the goals and objectives of the school be?

- What resources need to be applied to meet these objectives?

- How can these resources be most effectively and efficiently applied?

- How well have we met the school's goals and objectives?

- How can our answers to these questions guide our planning in the future?

These questions follow very closely the CIPP model described nearly a quarter of a century ago by Daniel Stufflebeam and his associates (1971). CIPP stands for *Context, Input, Process,* and *Product.* The first question above is a context question; it sets the direction for where the school is heading and what it will try to accomplish. The second question is an input question; i.e., "What personnel, material, and other resources need to be invested in the school program and at what points?" The third question addresses itself to process; it asks *how* we will apply the resources we have allocated. "What methods will teachers use to deliver instruction?" "How will we organize the school and its activities to best accomplish the goals and objectives that have been set?" The fourth question addresses the product of the educational program: "In terms of how we originally envisioned what we would like to accomplish, how successful have we been?" Finally, the fifth question reflects on the entire process and seeks direction for future planning. In doing this, we can revisit our questions in reverse order: "How well have we done in terms of our goals, and why have we succeeded or failed?" "How should we revise the way we do things in order to better serve our goals?" "What additional resources do we need?" ("Which do we no longer need?") "How should our goals be restated or revised?"

These questions will be raised throughout the chapters that follow on the planning process. For instance, Chapter 3 on the strategic planning process focuses most explicitly on the first question: "What should the goals and objectives of the school be?" But other considerations are important to strategic planning as well, such as when resources should be allocated, in what sequence should different procedures be instituted, who is responsible for what parts of the envisioned process, what costs will be incurred, what disruptions are likely, and what additional information is needed. An essential part of the strategic planning process is devising a strategy for learning about what is currently unknown (what you don't know *can* hurt you!) and making allowance for needed revisions, discovered through a pattern of constant monitoring.

In a similar manner, program evaluation is also a part of mid-range and short-range planning. Chapter 4 on mid-range planning focuses on annual goals and objectives, allocating resources and planning operational procedures to achieve them, and monitoring what is happening in order to improve plans for the future. Chapter 5 on short-range planning illustrates the same processes, though on a micro scale. All five questions we have raised are important at every level of planning, although greater emphasis is given to the first, fourth, and fifth questions in strategic planning and to the second and third questions in short-range planning. The monitoring and evaluation attitude that is embedded in all five questions is an essential ingredient of the planning process and builds upon a foundation to provide effective organizational oversight for the school that is described and developed in Chapter 2.

## A FINAL NOTE

As noted earlier, mastery of organizational oversight is necessary for scheduling, coordinating, and implementing the skills and knowledge associated with all the other domains. Leadership fails without direction, and direction implies planning. Written expression has a positive impact when it is coordinated with the purpose of the school; this implies planning and organizational oversight. Expertise in curriculum development must be coordinated with the goals and procedures of the school. Proper resource allocation is built on planning. Similar statements could be made regarding the skills and knowledge associated with each of the other domains. Without them, organizational oversight is empty, and without organizational oversight, these separate skills are uncoordinated. We encourage the principal to use this volume, not to build organizational oversight skills in isolation, but to integrate them with all the other facets of professional development.

# 2

# A FOUNDATION FOR ORGANIZATIONAL OVERSIGHT

A series of phrases comprises the National Policy Board for Educational Administration's definition of organizational oversight:

**Planning and scheduling** one's own and others' work so that resources are used appropriately and short- and long-term priorities and goals are met;

**Scheduling** flows of activities;

**Establishing** procedures to regulate activities;

**Monitoring** projects to meet deadlines;

**Empowering** the process in appropriate places.

The verbs introducing the first four phrases should sound very familiar to the veteran school administrator; they have been found in the literature on management and administration since at least 1900. The fifth phrase is introduced by the verb "empowering," a term that principals and other school administrators in the last decades of the twentieth century have heard with increasing frequency.

To some observers, "empowering" may seem somewhat inconsistent with the first four verbs: planning, scheduling, establishing, and monitoring. Traditionally, these four terms have been used primarily to strengthen the control of the person who is doing the planning, scheduling, establishing, and monitoring, and, as a result, to disempower others. However, we believe that while these terms speak to strengthening control, we do not believe that they necessarily require that anybody will lose power. We believe that when all stakeholders have a part in planning, scheduling, establishing, and monitoring, they are all empowered. The principal's competence in the organizational oversight domain will affect directly how empowered stakeholders become.

## TWO MODELS OF PROFESSIONAL ACTION

Argyris and Schön (1974, 1978) have articulated two models that describe the foundations, procedures, and outcomes of professional and organizational behavior patterns that empower or disempower organizational stakeholders. We will briefly present these two models here. Both models are described by their governing variables (i.e., the regular behaviors that represent implicit values), their action strategies, and their consequences. We will compare the two models in terms of these descriptive dimensions (Argyris & Schön, 1974):

*Governing Variables*

*Model I*

- Define goals and try to achieve them.
- Maximize winning and minimize losing.
- Minimize generating or expressing negative feelings.
- Be rational.

*Model II*

- Maximize valid information.
- Elicit free and informed choices.
- Develop internal commitment to the choice and constant monitoring of its implementation.

Looking down the list of governing variables associated with Model I, we discover the basis for much of the advice that traditionally has been given to school administrators by their colleagues and by university preparation programs. As we consider those associated with Model II, we see another list of behaviors that most principals and other school administrators would agree are desirable. However, the writings of Argyris and Schön, as well as other observers (Erlandson, 1976; Senge, 1990), make clear that for most principals (and other professionals) the governing variables of Model I take precedence over those of Model II in the actual behaviors that are demonstrated on the job. The different governing variables of the two models lead to different action strategies:

*Action Strategies*

| *Model I* | *Model II* |
|---|---|
| ◆ Design and manage the environment unilaterally. | ◆ Design situations or environments where participants can be origins and can experience high personal causation. |
| ◆ Own and control the task. | ◆ Jointly control tasks. |
| ◆ Unilaterally protect yourself. | ◆ Protect one's self and others bilaterally, with an orientation toward growth. |
| ◆ Unilaterally protect others from being hurt. | |

Note how for each model the action strategies flow directly from the underlying governing variables. Consider first the interactions that are likely to proceed from Model I. If I have stated a goal (e.g., "we will have the new core curriculum implemented by the end of the year") and value its attainment, then I will want to design and manage the environment in which it will be accomplished. I will work hard to persuade others to my way of thinking and of the necessity of accomplishing the goal for the overall good of the organization. If I see accomplishment of my goal as a reflection on myself and whether I have won or lost, I may let others participate in the implementation of the goal but I will maintain control of this task, lest the goal be subverted or altered. Since the expression of negative feelings can only interfere with the accomplishment of my goal, I will seek to suppress them by avoiding comments about specific behavior and covering up or denying incongruities between rhetoric and behavior. In a similar manner, I will attempt to manipulate the situation so that others are protected from attack and so that we may proceed on the task in a rational manner.

On the other hand, if I truly value the maximization of valid information so that all decisions can be best informed by data, I will seek to create situations and environments where others can be origins of data and goals and where their continued participation can be nurtured by their sense of high personal causation. Since I value both their insights and judgments, as well as their voluntary, enthusiastic participation in the process, I will welcome others into jointly controlling the task with me. Since both others and I value the opportunities that are made possible by our joint action and since we value the people in the process, we collaborate to see that each person in the process is protected.

Certain consequences flow from the two models, consequences both for the behavioral environment of the school and for learning:

*Consequences for the Behavioral Environment of the School*

| Model I | Model II |
|---|---|
| ◆ Principal seen as defensive, inconsistent, incongruent, competitive, controlling, fearful of being vulnerable, manipulative, withholding of feelings. | ◆ Principal seen as minimally defensive (facilitator, collaborator, choice creator). |
| ◆ Defensive interpersonal and group relationships. | ◆ Minimally defensive interpersonal relations and group dynamics. |
| ◆ Defensive norms. | ◆ Learning-oriented norms. |

The consequences for learning flow primarily from the fact that while Model II seeks valid information, Model I, because of its defensive norms, seeks to avoid new information that will question goals and strategies, threaten the principal's ownership and control of the process, or cause the expression of negative feelings. As a result, assumptions and beliefs are never tested openly or in terms of observable, disconfirmable data; usually they are tested privately and solely to confirm the original beliefs of the person who holds them. Data focus only on how well the articulated goals are being met, not on whether these articulated goals are optimal or even adequate. This is what Argyris and Schön call "single-loop" learning (i.e., a single feedback loop informs users only how well a plan of action has been implemented in terms of its stated goals). Model II, with different governing variables, different action strategies, and a different behavioral environment, produces very different consequences for learning. All procedures, beliefs, and theories are tested openly against common information and experience so that they can be confirmed or disconfirmed. Negative feelings are surfaced so that, like any other data, they can be tested and used to guide the process. "Double loop learning" provides feedback not only on how well goals are met but also on whether goals adopted in the past are still appropriate goals. The two models' different consequences for learning may be summarized as follows:

*Consequences for Learning*

| Model I | Model II |
|---------|----------|
| ◆ Self-sealing. | ◆ Disconfirmable processes. |
| ◆ Single-loop learning. | ◆ Double-loop learning. |
| ◆ Little public testing of theories; much private testing of theories. | ◆ Public testing of theories. |

Argyris and Schön demonstrate convincingly that in the long run and, especially in dealing with problematic questions, Model II increases effectiveness, but Model I decreases effectiveness. Two examples will help clarify the distinctions between Model I and Model II. Each of these examples represents a composite of real school situations that the authors have encountered.

## CREATING A MODEL I ENVIRONMENT

Audrey Smith is the principal of Bright Middle School. Through her participation in professional associations and graduate course work, she has become increasingly frustrated by the traditional, mundane, counterproductive educational program that operates in her school. Classes in her school emphasize rote memorization of facts and excessive drill in basic skills. Courses are organized according to the time-honored classifications of language arts, mathematics, science, and social studies. Even the "special" subjects, such as art and music, are taught in isolation from other courses. To make things worse, although her teachers complain about lazy, disruptive students and lack of support from parents, they apparently see no reason to change the basic organizational structure or focus of the school.

Audrey's frustration has reached its limits when she has the opportunity to spend two days observing a middle school in another state. Students in this middle school are excited about what's happening in their classes, are given considerable autonomy in structuring and achieving their own learning environments, and are eager to work on learning and to demonstrate the products of it. Courses in this school are hard to identify; teachers work cooperatively with each other in teams to examine the progress each child is making and to develop daily strategies for maximizing student growth. Parents are in the school regularly and work with teachers to enhance the school as a learning environment. Since the demographic characteristics of the school and its community are very similar to those of her own school, Audrey decides that this exciting learning environment can be achieved there also. She collects as much information as she can about the operation of the school so that she can reproduce it at Bright.

Since her visit has occurred fairly late in the spring, Audrey Smith takes no immediate action upon returning to Bright Middle School, other than letting her department chairpersons and other key faculty know that what she saw impressed her greatly and will have strong implications for the educational program at Bright. She spends the summer doing further research on middle school programs and corresponds often with the principal of the school she visited. She carefully plans the program she wishes to implement at Bright, and in August she calls her department chairs to school for a meeting so that she can share her blueprint for change with them.

Audrey is enthusiastic about her vision for the school, and her department chairs respond with similar enthusiasm to her well-orchestrated presentation. There

is much they don't understand in what she has presented, and some of what she proposes runs against
what they have believed and practiced over their
careers; but Audrey's enthusiasm is contagious and
they don't want to discourage her. They have a lot of
respect for Audrey Smith and know that she has
worked hard over the years to bring about renewal at
Bright. They want her to succeed. They each commend
Audrey on her presentation and wish her success in
initiating her ideas at Bright. Privately, however, each
chairperson has doubts, and in the parking lot as they
leave the school, they begin to share some of their
reservations with each other. Back in her office Audrey
inwardly rejoices that this first step has been so easy.

At a second meeting a week later Audrey asks if
any of the chairpersons sees any flaws in or has any
objections to what she has proposed. Several of the
chairs take this opportunity to identify some of their
concerns, but Audrey has anticipated them and offers
research and specific examples that support her proposed design for the school. She demonstrates easily
the fallacy of all objections, and when no further
concerns are raised, she turns very serious and tells
them that her plans cannot succeed without their
support. She solicits and receives a promise of support
from each of them.

Just prior to the opening of school, Audrey Smith
holds a faculty meeting to welcome back all her teachers and to tell them about her plans for the school. She
includes in her presentation her intention to do away
with a subject matter curriculum organized by departments and informs them that the current department
chairs will be working in pairs with interdisciplinary
groups to plan teaming efforts and to begin developing
the new curricula. She outlines a strategy for them to
follow and sets October 15 as a date for them to report
back on their separate group efforts to the entire
faculty.

The meeting on October 15 nearly devastates
Audrey. Plans for teaming reflect little more than a

division of labor that enables teachers to pursue their specialties with larger groups of students. Plans for the new curricula are little more than old wine in new bottles, carefully reflecting and respecting established subject matter boundaries and time parameters. Proposals for evaluation make unsatisfactory gestures to "real world" learnings and higher order thinking. She listens with growing internal frustration but with an unruffled demeanor. When the last of the reports has been delivered, she calmly tells her teachers that she knows they are trying hard but that their planning has been much too mundane and has not significantly addressed the critical issues of middle school education. She promises to give them additional guidance and to work with each of their groups personally.

From the October meeting until the December break Audrey Smith strives valiantly to keep her promise. She attends nearly every team meeting and works hard with the designated team leaders to try to get them on track and to begin developing a curriculum that truly meets the needs of young adolescents. She patiently repeats and documents the need for change, and when her pleas bring forth no significant alternatives, she generates her own. She is convinced that it would have been easier to rewrite the entire curriculum and define team procedures herself. "Why," she asks herself, "are things so difficult at Bright Middle School?" Were things this difficult at the middle school she had observed? Her conversations with the principal of that school didn't seem to indicate that they were. Are her teachers less capable? Prior to this year she had always been convinced that her teachers were markedly above average. Perhaps she was wrong.

Audrey takes the opportunity afforded by the holiday break to assess the overall progress of her initiative at Bright. She realizes that by any objective standard she has made very little progress. The teachers have generally complied with her wishes, but they are obviously no longer very enthusiastic about the school renewal that she is seeking. This puzzles Audrey. After all, all the department chairs have pledged their support to the process, and she has answered all the teachers' objections to it. Also, while the teachers have at times expressed their frustration in trying to meet her demands, they have never openly criticized her efforts. Maybe things will be different when school resumes in January.

Things do indeed change in the new year, but not as Audrey hoped they would. Teachers increasingly miss team meetings, and many meetings have to be canceled. When she tries to remind them of their commitment, she is met with hostility. She fares no better when she tries to call in the promises of support that her department chairpersons have given her. They tell her that while what she is doing is theoretically correct and is probably working very well in another middle school in another state, it doesn't really fit so neatly at Bright. They also tell her that she is trying to bring about too much change too fast. When Audrey appeals to the superintendent and the central office staff, she receives similar responses. By April she is a very discouraged principal, not sure where she went wrong and seriously considering returning to the classroom.

## CREATING A MODEL II ENVIRONMENT

Daniel Garcia is the principal of Woods Middle School, the middle school where Audrey Smith received her inspiration for renewal of her own school. Daniel took over as principal four years ago to correct a situation that was characterized by high student absenteeism, high student and teacher turnover, low teacher morale, and very low student scores on standardized tests. It was his first principalship, and he accepted the position eagerly, though he knew that Woods would be a very difficult school to change. Daniel had been selected for the position because of his own record at Woods as a very successful, if somewhat unconventional, teacher. At the time of his appointment, several school board members and a number of the district administrators expressed doubts about his

ability to function as a principal. But the superintendent was desperate and knew that desperate measures
were needed. And the risk was low: Woods couldn't
get much worse.

Daniel had doubted his own abilities too. He had
his own ideas about what was needed to make middle
school kids succeed; but he knew also that most teachers did not look favorably on some of his methods, at
least not as models for their own teaching. Most of his
fellow teachers, in fact, did admire Daniel profession-
ally for what he had accomplished, and they also
admired him personally because of his openness and
because of his willingness to learn and to talk frankly
about his classroom failures as well as his successes.
Nevertheless, Daniel had never directed his colleagues
before, and he was more than a little nervous as that
first school year began.

At the first faculty meeting of the year, just prior to
the opening of school in August, Daniel Garcia openly
shared his fears and reservations with the faculty. At
the same time he painted a vivid picture of the situation at Woods, a picture with which they were all too
familiar. He made it clear that he didn't have the
answers; but he presented to them his deepest beliefs
about what the students needed and how those needs
could be fulfilled. The faculty responded with their
own ideas, many of which were contrary to Daniel's;
but because of the precedent he had set by honestly
presenting his own positions and his reasons for them,
their responses followed the same pattern. The discussion grew heated at times and emotion, rather than
reason, clearly drove many of the statements that were
made. However, even those teachers who were usually
withdrawn and silent at meetings took part in the
discussion. The meeting went a half hour past the
announced dismissal time. Daniel had to work to bring
the discussion to a close. Though nothing concrete had
been accomplished, several teachers commented on
their way to the parking lot that it was the best meeting

they had ever had. One of the older teachers said, in reference to Daniel: "He's going to be okay."

Daniel and the teachers spent the first few months of that school year gaining an honest and comprehensive assessment of the situation at Woods Middle School. The picture that was painted was fairly dismal, and teachers saw for the first time that many of the best things they thought they were doing were having little positive impact on the students. However, Daniel urged them to not to sell themselves short, to look at their strengths and see how they could capitalize on them. Next, the faculty began to build a vision. Because of the pressures that had been put upon them, much of their thinking was circumscribed by standardized test scores. But Daniel and a gradually increasing number of teachers urged their colleagues to look beyond those scores and ask what they ultimately wanted for the students at Woods Middle School. The faculty as a whole began to see that test scores, at best, represented benchmarks of their progress toward more lofty goals for which they had no reliable measures. This produced a sense of awe at the scope of the task they had taken on; but it also produced a growing unity in the faculty and a sense that they could learn from each other, an invaluable resource that they could no longer afford to ignore.

Not everyone on the faculty was won over immediately. Many of the best and brightest teachers held out against the changes for a long time. But a learning climate had been established in which it was safe to present alternatives to either traditional or proposed courses of action. These teachers learned that they could openly test the principal's or anyone else's ideas but that their own ideas would also be tested. These holdouts began to back up their ideas with research, observation, and logic, and their proposals became incorporated into the evolving school program. As they saw their proposals make an impact on the course of the school, they gradually became caught up in the vision of the school and many became its strongest supporters.

Now, four years since Daniel Garcia became principal, Woods Middle School has become a very different school. Formerly, large numbers of teachers petitioned to be transferred out of Woods; now they are fighting to be transferred into it. Student absenteeism and truancy problems have virtually been eliminated. Parents want their students in school, and they want their students in *this* school. Parents themselves are caught up in the learning ethic, not only for their children but for themselves as well. They make provisions at home for students to do their homework, and they themselves have expanded their own reading habits. Some who could not read have gone to school at night to learn to read. Many are in the school regularly during the school day to assist teachers and secretarial staff. The school has truly become theirs. And the whole school organization has gradually changed. Teachers who know that they need each other's insights are working together, often across subject matter lines, to assist students in their learning. They themselves have become eager learners, and they have become involved in each other's, as well as students', learning. The entire school has become a learning environment. And, almost incidentally and without paying much attention to them, standardized test scores have gone up.

Daniel Garcia is happy with what has occurred at Woods Middle School, but he is not satisfied. He feels there is still a lot to accomplish at Woods. What he feels best about is that the atmosphere of hopelessness that greeted him when he became principal at Woods has disappeared. Failures still occur, but they are seen as learning opportunities. Some teachers have still not entirely bought into the Woods vision; but the climate of the school demands reasoned proposals supported by evidence, and as these teachers meet this criterion, they find that their initiatives are also contributing to growth. Slowly, they are becoming full contributing members of the Woods team. Daniel has never been so busy, but he has never before enjoyed his work so much. It is exciting to come to work each day.

Over the course of his first year on the job, Daniel Garcia built a cohesive team of teachers, parents, and students. Audrey Smith did not. From the beginning of that first year, Daniel Garcia demonstrated a hunger for alternatives. Audrey Smith did not. Daniel Garcia invited others to generate ideas and gain ownership in the process. Audrey Smith did not. Daniel Garcia encouraged the public testing of alternatives for the school's program. Audrey Smith did not. Throughout their respective first years, Daniel Garcia promoted organizational behavior that Argyris and Schön classify as Model II, and Audrey Smith ensured, by her words and actions, that the organization would follow Model I.

## IMPLICATIONS FOR ORGANIZATIONAL OVERSIGHT

Schools in America are "flat" organizations, meaning that there are few levels in the organizational hierarchy of a typical American school. There are usually only two real levels: the principal and everyone else. Even in most cases where one or more assistant principals exist, these positions do not insulate the principal from contact with every teacher in the school, to say nothing of other professionals, such as counselors and librarians, or such classified staff as secretaries, custodians, and lunch workers. There are some exceptions to this, notably in *some* large high schools; but even in these cases, the principal has a "span of control" that would be considered unacceptable, if not impossible, in most other employment sectors. This organizational situation also distinguishes the American principal from his/her counterparts in some other developed nations. A colleague from England shook his head in disbelief when he discovered that, in a group of fairly typical American elementary schools, each principal had 50 to 75 persons reporting directly to her.

Given the increasing claims that are being placed on the educational dollar, it is not likely that the situation will change drastically in the immediate future. Even if it were possible, it might not be prudent to insulate the principal further from teachers and their classrooms by installing additional layers of bureaucracy. As we shall see later in this chapter, there are some strong reasons to believe that increasing the managerial hierarchy would tend to produce more Model I behavior, with the result that schools would be even less adept in responding to their environments or to the problems that occur in them.

If, on the other hand, a school is truly converted into a Model II environment, the principal is no longer alone in the business of planning, scheduling, establishing, or monitoring. Every teacher, secretary, custodian, parent, and student who has joined in determining the destiny of the school is now a source of additional information, another set of eyes and ears to monitor the implementation of the plan that guides that destiny, and another source of energy to make it work. The plan is self-renewing because valid data are focused on real questions and problems, and theories and assumptions are publicly tested. An atmosphere is developed that supports the entire organizing process.

Peter Senge (1990) has made the point that:

> ...personal vision, by itself, is not the key to more effective creativity. The key is "creative tension," the tension between vision and reality. The most effective people are those who can "hold" their vision while remaining committed to seeing current reality clearly. This principle is no less true for organizations. The hallmark of a learning organization is not lovely visions floating in space, but a relentless willingness to examine "what is" in light of our vision. (p. 226)

## JOHN F. KENNEDY HIGH SCHOOL

John F. Kennedy, in the Bronx, New York, is a large, comprehensive, inner-city high school that Sara Lightfoot (1983) portrayed as being exceptionally responsive to its environment and to the needs of its students. This school acquired a reputation for excellence in its early years under principal Bob Mastruzzi even though it was a regular New York City high school, without designated magnet programs or special funding. Although many of its students came to the school from some of the most socioeconomically disadvantaged neighborhoods in America, John F. Kennedy High

School developed a reputation for excellence in academics, athletics, and the fine arts. Daily attendance rates were consistently well above the average for other city schools, and faculty and student morale were high. The school also developed a reputation as a caring institution, much of it resulting from the personal emphasis given that dimension by the principal. Lightfoot records a statement made by Bob Mastruzzi to the school's graduating seniors:

> "I don't care if you are going to Columbia University pre-med, or if you have been tops in our Honors program. If you don't give a bit of yourself to someone else, you are a failure!" (p. 118)

However, John F. Kennedy High School was not a one-man show, though Bob Mastruzzi was clearly the dominant factor in the school. One of the authors had the good fortune, as a college professor in New York City, to work closely with Bob when the school opened in 1972. Bob selected his faculty, particularly his assistant principals and department chairs, for their strong character and intellect. After only a few minutes in one of his cabinet meetings, it was evident that these bright, independent individuals did not all agree with each other and were not afraid to express their disagreement. But they respected each other's ability, and they were willing to examine facts and assumptions openly. The author also observed that it was acceptable to be wrong and to change one's mind when the facts supported a different conclusion. In the many days that the author spent at the school, it became apparent that this same attitude toward data-driven decisions trickled down from the top to nearly every area of the school program. The author retains his conviction that the success of John F. Kennedy High School was a direct result of this process—a process in which it was safe to present divergent opinions and legitimate to test them publicly.

## HOLLIBROOK ELEMENTARY SCHOOL

The same author has had the opportunity to get acquainted with Hollibrook Elementary School, in Houston, Texas, and to get to know its former principal, Suzanne Still, and a number of its faculty. Hollibrook has also received considerable recognition for excellence—a reputation based largely upon outstanding academic achievement by students from poor minority families. Nearly all the students come from families receiving federal and state assistance; many come from families where little English is spoken. Before Suzanne Still arrived as principal, the school had become notorious for its low academic achievement. But the school, inspired by this visionary principal, refused to accept that its students could not learn. Parents, teachers, secretaries, and the principal were committed to the belief that the students should learn both academic and life skills and that together they could make it possible for them to do so. Once again, the principal was the driving force, but ideas and support came from everyone. Once freed to use their own creativity there was almost no limit to what they could do to enhance the educational experience of the children.

However, it is clear that the school's success in driving up student achievement, reinvigorating faculty, and gaining the active participation of parents was not simply a function of wide open freedom for teachers or of an empty collaborative process in which individuals begin to feel better about themselves and others. As the faculty focused on the areas of (1) teaching and the improvement of instruction, (2) professional leadership, and (3) organizational leadership, current performance was openly tested against theory and research, and shaped by open experimentation. The willingness to learn from observing and openly discussing current practice, in terms of its impact on performance, proved to be an invigorating tonic for the entire school organization and its stakeholders. Hollibrook provides an excellent example of a Model II organization. It also evokes memories of the open experimentation that occurred in an earlier Model II school, the laboratory school of John Dewey that operated about 100 years ago (Mayhew & Edwards, 1936).

These two schools stand as examples of what can be accomplished when a Model II environment prevails. But they are not completely isolated examples. Similar schools can be found nationwide. However, it is true that the vast majority of schools still remain as Model I environments. Perhaps unfortunately, Model I schools do not go out of existence. Since "planning," "scheduling," "establishing," and "monitoring" are seen apart from empowerment, what usually happens is that these schools continue, deprived of much valid information and the personal investment of many of their most able stakeholders. The principal who would lay the basis for a strong organization, an organization in which implementation is energized and monitored by everyone—not just the principal or a few key individuals—should consider taking steps toward creating a Model II environment.

## TRANSITION TO A MODEL II ENVIRONMENT

After all we have said about the virtues of a Model II environment, we will have to admit that the transition to such an environment will not be an easy one. The pseudo-rationality that is embedded in Model I behavior is such a powerful part of our culture and our professional roles that it will not be easily dislodged. Even a principal who fully understands the dynamics of Model I and Model II behaviors and is fully aware of their consequences for school effectiveness will still have a difficult time effecting a transition to Model II.

A major part of the problem is the internal contradiction in the statement: "The principal will develop a Model II environment at his school." It should be clear to the reader from what was written earlier that this statement implies that the principal will take on the personal goal of changing the school in a specific direction. As stated, the task is an admirable overarching goal that the principal owns and will want to achieve. This is clearly reflective of Model I behavior, which will inevitably result in reciprocal Model I behaviors on the part of other school stakeholders and thus deny attainment of the very goal that was stated. There is no allowance that this goal may be modified or even diverted in a different direction based upon valid input from other stakeholders.

This, of course, presents the principal with a genuine dilemma. If the goal of attaining a Model II environment may be subverted by the Model II process, what is the use of pursuing it? If, on the other hand, a Model II environment is pursued by Model I methods, its validity is denied. The solution is to treat Model II as a hypothesis (not as an articulated goal) and to test it through Model II procedures. If valid information, free and informed choice, and internal commitment produce a world that is different from what one would expect a Model II world to be, the foundations of Model II would predict that it would be a better one. In fact, in our experience with this process, a Model II world is produced when Model II procedures are consistently applied.

We would reiterate our strong belief that effective organizational oversight requires a Model II environment. The first step in the transition is for the principal to fully understand what is involved. If the principal feels less than fully certain after reading what has been presented in this chapter, we would recommend that he/she begin by examining the writings of Argyris and Schön, particularly their 1974 book, *Theory in Practice: Increasing Professional Effectiveness*.

Then the principal should make a careful assessment of where the school is in terms of a Model II environment. One way of doing this is to administer a survey form, similar to that presented in Figure 2.1, to teachers, parents, and other school stakeholders.

A caveat needs to be added here about this survey: the survey will never lead to Model II outcomes if Model I procedures are used to administer it. Obviously, the survey needs to be confidential, but much needs to be done beyond this. The principal needs to take care, before distributing it, to carefully explain (in person, not in a written format) why he/she is using it. Legitimately this should be a simple, plainly worded admission that the principal is not sure that teachers (or other stakeholders) have adequate access to either the school's decision-making processes or to information about the bases for these decisions. The principal should honestly admit that it may not be as open a process as it ought to be and that he/she is seeking ways to improve it. The principal should describe the instrument itself, pointing out that it was kept simple to make it easy to complete, but encouraging additional open-ended responses from any person who wants to take the time to make them. The principal should ask for volunteers to help review the returned questionnaires, ensuring that all major subgroups of the school's stakeholders (and major factions within those subgroups) are represented in the group that will assist in the review. The principal should promise feedback in a timely fashion.

## FIGURE 2.1. INFORMATION AND DECISIONS AT WASHINGTON ELEMENTARY SCHOOL: A SURVEY

|  |  | Yes | Uncertain | No |
|---|---|---|---|---|
| 1. | I play an important part in how policies are made and carried out in the school. | Y | U | N |
| 2. | Decisions in the school are made on the basis of evidence that supports educational goals, not on the basis of personal preferences. | Y | U | N |
| 3. | I have access to all the information I need about how the school operates in regard to: |  |  |  |
|  | a.  Budget | Y | U | N |
|  | b.  Curriculum | Y | U | N |
|  | c.  Student personnel | Y | U | N |
|  | d.  Staff evaluation | Y | U | N |
|  | e.  Staff development | Y | U | N |
| 4. | How, specifically, could the school decision-making be made more open? |  |  |  |
| 5. | Other comments: |  |  |  |

Another danger will arise when the survey results are examined. It's always hard to receive news that seems to reflect negatively on one's performance. It's especially hard when the news is received in the company of one's coworkers, and it's perhaps even harder when that news seems to be the result of misperceptions. In such cases it is very difficult not to become defensive. During this review process and in all stages that follow, the principal needs to keep in mind that his/her purpose is to maximize valid information. Opinion (whether the principal's or someone else's) needs to be considered as opinion. The principal doesn't have to prove anything about his/her performance. What the principal needs to do is to find out what is in fact happening by testing all opinions (including the principal's own) against the facts. The principal's behavior in this survey review process will do much to set the tone for future transactions.

The same attitude and behavior should prevail in all subsequent transactions. Following review by the committee, the survey results should be presented to the stakeholders who have responded. Subsequently, representatives of the stakeholders need to work together to design tentative strategies for transforming the school. These tentative strategies then need to be shared with all stakeholders. The process of formulating tentative strategies, testing, and reformulating should continue as an ongoing process.

## DEVELOPING A STRUCTURE FOR ORGANIZATIONAL OVERSIGHT

Formal communication in American schools typically runs down from the principal and back up to the principal. As we have noted, because schools are "flat" organizations, particularly at the elementary school level, the principal tends to be flooded with communications about all types of problems and demands for decisions. Even in a complex secondary school the basic pattern is essentially the same. While there may be a host of assistants and department chairs and communications of consequence may travel through many separate channels, they all converge at one point at the top: the principal. As a result, the principal, rather than being confronted with a single problem, receives fragmentary and often conflicting pieces of data from many sources in regard to a single problem. Traditionally, then, the principal weighs the conflicting evidence before handing down a decision that he/she hopes will satisfy the problem. This mode of decision making tends to set the principal above other members of the organization, to isolate the principal from the other persons in the organization, and, consequently, to promote a Model I organizational environment.

As we have noted, the problem will not be solved simply by adding assistant principals or specialists, such as counselors, librarians, or social workers. In fact, given the traditional organization of the school, the addition of these persons usually exacerbates the problem. Adding assistants and specialists to the bureaucracy does not change the basic communication flow that is at the heart of the organization. Information still flows up (though now it is filtered to make it more manageable), and decisions flow down.

"Delegation" of authority to an assistant may make the job of the principal less oppressive, but it does little to change the basic organizational structure. While overall responsibility is made more manageable when pieces of it are delegated, there is also the danger that such delegation may further separate the principal from direct contact with the human elements of the organization. Information that flows down from the principal is filtered through the persons to whom particular areas of responsibility have been delegated. Information that flows upward goes through the same filtering process. Thus, the principal is faced with a dilemma. A situation where 50 or more people have direct access to seek information from the principal and furnish information to the principal is an impossible one and promises to destroy planning and other organizational functions. Yet when the information is filtered to make it more manageable, it tends to further isolate the principal from the organization's stakeholders.

The traditional organizational chart (see Fig. 2.2) describes a linear pattern of communication flow that typifies the problem. As information and decisions flow up and down the

---

**FIGURE 2.2. AN ORGANIZATION CHART REPRESENTING A PERSON-TO-PERSON PATTERN OF ORGANIZATION**

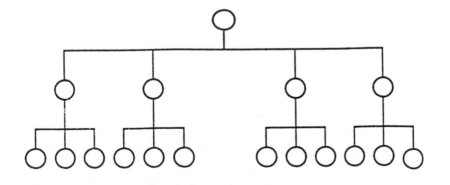

---

organizational structure, each route may become isolated from those that are running parallel to it, leading to the principal's receiving requests and information that are fragmentary and conflicting. Effective principals have always found ways to work around these limitations, making certain that they get information directly from teachers, students, and parents so that they are able to evaluate the information and requests that they receive appropriately. However, the basic organizational structure is still at the root of their problem unless they take direct action to alter it.

Years ago, Rensis Likert described an alternative to the traditional person-to-person pattern of organization. This overlapping workgroup form of organization (see Fig. 2.3) emphasizes building small, effective workgroups that each possess a "high degree of group loyalty, effective skills of interaction, and high performance goals." Likert asserts that such groups will enhance group members' motivation to (1) accept the goals and decisions of the group, (2) seek to influence the goals and decisions of the group so that they are consistent with their own experiences and goals, (3) communicate fully with other group members, and (4) help implement group goals and decisions (Likert, 1961, pp. 104–105). Principals should cast groups carefully, assigning overlapping memberships as a means of knitting groups together. Likert suggests that those with leadership roles in one group might follow in others.

## TEAM LEADERSHIP

One of the most effective ways to transform a school into a Model II environment and to build an organizational structure based upon overlapping work groups is to work through a campus leadership team. The use of a team by the principal is at once a confession that he or she cannot do the job of organizing and leading the school alone and a strategy for modeling, on a smaller, seminal scale, the principles of trust and interdependence that the principal wishes to infuse into the entire school organization. The organization process is empowered at appropriate places by directing empowerment first to those persons, who by virtue of personality, position, or tradition, are the human keys to the school's organizational structure and culture.

In recent years much has been written and said about campus leadership teams. We do not wish to review that entire

FIGURE 2.3. AN ORGANIZATION CHART DEPICTING AN OVERLAPPING GROUP FORM OF ORGANIZATION

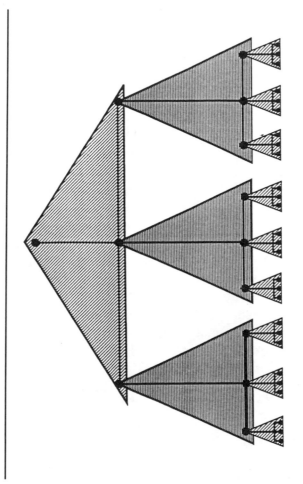

literature or the arguments that have been made for various types of team arrangements. Our concern here is focused on the formation of a team for purposes of providing organizational oversight in a way that enlists and empowers all stakeholders in that oversight and facilitates the communication flow between them. Schools are complex human organizations and are, consequently, prime candidates for all the problems of disarray and dysfunction that plague such organizations. A campus team, to assist the principal in overseeing the organization of the school, can be a powerful first step toward solving those problems.

How should such a team be formed? What is its purpose? How should it operate? How should it relate to all the school's stakeholders? First, we should note that the "leadership team" is not an alternative to the overlapping group type of organization described by Likert. The principal who merely trades the authoritarian control of an individual for the authoritarian control of an elite group has gained nothing and has perhaps added confusion at the top of the organization and multiplied resentment throughout it. However, the team should be the core of the new organization and should demonstrate the work group style and atmosphere that will hopefully permeate the restructured organization. Membership on the team should be sufficiently constant to provide continuity and to foster the establishment of internal interpersonal working relationships. At the same time it should be sufficiently open and changing so that new members may be added on a permanent or temporary basis to respond to new circumstances.

The principal should form the team in a way that reflects the envisioned organizational structure. Beyond this, there is no simple formula for constituting the team, and each school situation will require a different arrangement. However, certain principles apply. Obviously, key communicators in the organization should be included. Some of these persons will be essential because of their formal position in the organization (e.g., assistant principal or department chair); others will be important because of their personalities and the personal organizational links they have established. Both types of persons should be included on the team. Sandra McCalla, the very successful principal of Captain Shreve High School in

Shreveport, Louisiana, conducted a study of communications in her faculty to determine "who talks to whom about what" (McCalla, 1987). Her study confirmed much of what she already assumed, but there were also a number of surprises. Her study and later practice revealed that by talking directly with just three key communicators, she could effectively transmit her message to sixty percent of the faculty in a very short period of time. She noted that this was a better rate than if she had announced it at a faculty meeting!

The team should be representative of all stakeholding groups; it should not be monopolized by one group or a few groups. Obviously, the different segments (and factions) of the faculty should be included; but, in addition, parents and other school stakeholders should be members of this team. Not every work group in the school needs to be represented on the team (this will vary depending on the size of the school and other factors), but each should have easy access for communication to the team. This access should be built in through overlapping group memberships. Also, care should be taken to ensure that major divergent points of view are represented on the team. One of the chief purposes of the team is to deal with controversy in an open, mutually productive fashion that sets a tone for the entire school. Provision should also be made for temporary membership on the team. In response to particular problems or in anticipation of particular events or programs, persons with particular expertise should be made members of the group. Whether these ad hoc appointments become permanent or not is a decision that can be made by the team and the individuals involved.

Above all, the primary task of the team is to work with the principal to create an effective organization. Much has been written over the years about the nature of effective organizations. This includes work by early writers such as Likert (1961, 1967) and Argyris and Schön (1974, 1978), as well as recent contributions by writers like Senge (1990), Sergiovanni (1992), Leithwood (1993), and Fullan (1993). The principal and team who wish to restructure their organization would be well advised to consult these sources and to consider carefully the principles they propose. However, the primary work of restructuring the school organization must be the creative activity of persons within the school itself. This is the primary mission of the leadership team. They must first of all make the team an effective work group, built upon trust and mutual support. Team members must then carry the principles of effective group functioning back into the work groups of which they are members. Their goal is to create an organization in which effective, productive communication flows freely within and between all groups. If they accomplish this goal, most of their other priorities will fall into place rather neatly. The team must be an infectious carrier of the Model II ethic to the entire organization.

Examples of effective teams can be seen in the operation of effective schools. Earlier we briefly described the ways that two schools, John F. Kennedy High School and Hollibrook Elementary School, used Model II environments to build organizations that were responsive to their stakeholders. Both of these schools effectively used teams (though the term "team" was not often used) to promote these environments. In John F. Kennedy the team was structured primarily along formal organizational lines. Yet, individuals in formal positions of leadership (primarily the assistant principals and department chairs, but also other key individuals) had been recruited for both excellence and diversity and developed a model of group functioning that permeated the entire school, allowing for both necessary regularity and productive creativity throughout the school's operation (Lightfoot, 1983). By contrast, Suzanne Still at Hollibrook, confronted with a deteriorating situation that required radical corrective measures, built a looser, more informal core team, enlisting faculty, staff, and parents who shared her vision for organization renewal and educational excellence. The dynamism of this expanding team continued to win new converts from the school's various stakeholding groups and gradually permeated the entire school organization.

At both Kennedy and Hollibrook, effective team working environments were built upon mutual respect, trust, and support. These working environments, in turn, fostered effective communication flow. As noted earlier, the members of Bob Mastruzzi's cabinet would argue heatedly with each other in the process of constructing a plan of action that all would support. Bob made it clear that their divergent opinions were encouraged and expected. His own habit of "undefensive self-criticism" (Lightfoot, p. 71) generated reciprocal behaviors. Though not always achieved, the goal of valid communication among all groups of students, teachers, parents, and community members gave direction to the team and the entire school. Similarly, trust was the foundation of the Hollibrook experience. Teachers learned that the principal trusted them, and they, in turn, learned to trust the principal and each other. Teachers demonstrated a willingness to learn from their mistakes. Open communication became the standard, not only within the faculty, but also among teachers, students, staff, parents, and the community.

Senge (1990) has reiterated and built upon the work of Argyris and his colleagues to make a number of important observations related to the learning and development of teams. He notes that there "has never been a greater need for mastering team learning in organizations than there is today" (p. 236). This is so because the complexity of modern organizations and the impact of the information age require teams to translate complicated individual knowledge and decisions into organizational action. He identifies three critical dimensions for team learning:

♦ *A need to think insightfully about complex issues.*
  Within an organization there is a tendency to reduce diverse thoughts to the lowest common denominator. The team has the resources to ensure that the collective intelligence of the team is more, not less, than the contributions of its individual members. These resources need to be developed.

♦ *A need for innovative, coordinated action.*
  Outstanding teams build a bond of trust between team members that enables members to act in spontaneous yet coordinated ways.

♦ *A need for team members to foster learning in other teams.*
  In an overlapping group form of organization, leadership team members are also members of other teams. Through exercise of their teaming skills they foster similar norms and practices in other teams.

The first need of the team (to think thoughtfully about complex issues and thereby expand the collective intelligence of the team) relates closely to the first governing principle of Model II behavior: maximize valid information. The learning team uses both discussion and dialogue in expanding its collective intelligence. In "discussion," different views are presented and defended by those who hold them. By contrast, "dialogue" goes beyond any one individual's understanding. No one is trying to win in a dialogue. What is sought is an expanded common meaning that brings all team members beyond the understanding that they had separately.

The second requirement of the learning team is to create a base for innovative, coordinated action. As we have noted, both discussion and dialogue are needed to move the leadership team and the organization forward. To achieve this a bond of trust must be developed between team members that will diminish defensive behavior and allow productive interaction between discussion and dialogue. In this atmosphere, alternative views are presented and aired, and by an agreed upon process of team analysis are compared and combined to create a new meaning and understanding that can be translated into action.

Finally, the leadership team must, primarily through its members' involvement on other teams, foster productive team behavior throughout the organization. Once the leadership team itself has truly become a learning team, its learning can be infused throughout the organization. But becoming a learning team does not occur naturally or easily. It takes practice. As Senge says, "Learning teams learn how to learn together" (p. 257). Senge goes on to state:

> If anything, team skills are *more* challenging to develop than individual skills. This is why learning teams need "practice fields," ways to practice together so that they can develop their collective learning skills. The almost total absence of meaningful "practice" or "rehearsal" is probably the predominant factor that keeps most maagement teams from being effective learning units. (p. 258)

Senge recommends dialogue sessions to allow a team to come together to practice the skills of dialogue. These dialogue skills, which are relatively undeveloped in most persons, can be built by establishing the ground rules for practice sessions and coming together to practice dialogue just as an athletic team would come together for practice. The proposed guidelines for practice follow very closely those that are suggested by Argyris and Schön for the development of Model II behavior. Critical in these practice sessions are the ability and willingness to raise "difficult, subtle, and conflictual issues essential to the team's work" (Senge, p. 260). The team must learn to recognize and acknowledge when it is discussing rather than dialoging. These are difficult skills, and the team must use its practice sessions to develop them.

Although practice sessions are designed primarily to build longrange team skills, they can be used to address real problems. Even while these team skills are in their early stages of development, they can be most effectively practiced and monitored while they are being applied to the team's ongoing work.

Sergiovanni (1992) has proposed that the entire concept of "organization" is an inadequate one to guide schools and should be replaced by the concept of "community." "Organization," he believes, has been inappropriately transferred from the corporate sector of our society. Organizations are artificial structures that interfere with the natural supportive interactions that are developed in a community, whose members are guided by a common vision and whose futures are intertwined with each other.

Like Sergiovanni, we find the ideal of "community" an appealing one for schools. The problem we see with his proposal is that true communities develop naturally. By contrast, the school is an artificial structure, a somewhat arbitrary and artificial assembly of people created and mandated by the government. As a result, while we would certainly welcome the transformation of a school into a community, we must recognize that it takes time to build "community" in a school.

To build community, the principal needs to plan and create a structure that enhances open two-way communication among all stakeholders of the school. Such a structure will build community; a structure that inhibits open two-way comunication will destroy it. The principal's development of a campus leadership team for the school is central to this process.

The best form for a leadership team will differ from school to school and will vary with the requirements of the school and the special mix of people that inhabit and support it (principal, teachers, other professionals, students, parents, secretaries, etc.). The principal who wishes to move his/her school to a Model II organization will give priority to identifying and developing this core group of individuals who can, together with the principal, begin working toward a pervasive Model II culture. This practice of progressively moving toward a Model II environment in the school provides a necessary foundation for the strategic planning process that is discussed in Chapter 3.

## ACTION FOLLOW-UP

◆ Use the survey form presented in Figure 2.1 to make an assessment of where your school stands with respect to a Model I or Model II environment. Use this information in collaboration with the key stakeholders of the school to make recommendations for moving the school toward a Model II environment. Act on these recommendations.

◆ Tentatively identify persons who you believe would be appropriate members of a leadership team for your school. Identify the reasons for inclusion of each of these individuals. Share your team plan with two or more of the key members you have identified. Work with them to further develop the membership and mission of the team.

◆ Work with the team members you have identified to draft an organizational structure that will enhance the development of a Model II environment. Include in your plan a design for fostering team-building skills throughout the school.

◆ Begin using your regular team meetings as dialogue sessions. On a rotating basis, assign team members the responsibility for keeping track of when the group is discussing and when it is dialoging and how effectively it is functioning as a team (in terms of the three critical dimensions for team learning). Obtain feedback from the team member assigned this responsibility as a regular feature of each team meeting.

# 3

# STRATEGIC PLANNING

Strategic planning is long-range planning. The principal who would engage in it for guiding the course of the school has a problem. The environment of the school is turbulent, and society itself is changing at an unprecedented rate. The future for which the school is preparing the student will be different from the present. That's nearly the only thing that can be said about it with any certainty. The primary jobs for which schools are preparing students may be nearly obsolete in the next decade. The legal-governmental structure in which schools operate in the future may be very different from the one in which they operate today. Even a bet on the "basic skills" is not a sure thing, because the definition of literacy is changing rapidly and new "basic skills" are emerging. "Computer literacy" has moved to the fore, but even the meaning of this phrase is changing constantly. A child without fluency in a second language may be at a very real disadvantage in the twenty-first century. The problem is that although we know that the requirements for our students' future welfare are changing, we don't know for certain what the new requirements will be. This makes strategic planning very difficult for the school.

The principal faces a dilemma that is not helped much by traditional models of problem solving. The classical model follows a very straightforward, logical path. *Problem Identification* leads to *Problem Analysis*. This, in turn, leads to a generation of all possible *Alternatives* and an examination of the *Consequences* of each of the alternatives. This enables an *Evaluation* of the alternatives in terms of objectives, resulting in the *Selection* and *Implementation* of the best alternative (Hoy &Tarter, 1995). The problem is that the principal never has perfect knowledge of all alternatives, of their consequences, or even of the criteria by which they are to be judged. Even problem identification and analysis are never perfect. In turbulent modern society, with a multiplied availability of rich and varied data, the problem is intensified. Executives, including principals, who seek out all possible information, are likely to drown in it.

What does the principal do? At best, the principal probably makes the same compromise that is made by executives and managers in other organizations: he/she finds a solution that, while not optimum, appears "good enough" (Hoy & Tarter, 1995). The search for a solution that will "work" tends to cause the principal (or other executive or administrator) to ignore many of the implications of the larger world and focus only on the narrow objectives by which he/she is evaluated. For instance, there has been a tremendous emphasis on reading and mathematics literacy in recent years, with literacy defined by standardized tests. While one can easily make a case that the basic skills of reading and mathematics are indeed essential, their identification as the essence of literacy and the quantitative nature of their assessment have often allowed them to become the necessary and sufficient indicators of success.

A few years ago an elementary principal and a group of her teachers proudly told one of the authors (a university professor) that their school's vision was that "all students will be on grade level in reading and mathematics by the end of the fifth grade." The author's response was that in his entire adult life he had never been asked if he were on grade level at the end of fifth grade or any other grade. His purpose in saying this was not to minimize the importance of reading and mathematics but to point out that these achievements were only means to an end—the goal of a personally and socially productive life—that encompassed so much more than adequacy in these two skill areas. The problem is that other essential ingredients (the ability to successfully deal with racism; the ability to form strong, lasting, productive interpersonal relationships; etc.) are problematic in their definitions and are much more difficult to measure. Also, the principal's administrative superiors will probably not assess her so rigorously on these outcomes even if they realize their importance, because they, like the principal, have no ready way to do so. Does this make these outcomes less important? No. Does it make them more likely to be effectively ignored? Yes.

Hoy and Tarter (1995) observe that, in fact, many school administrators fall short of even a limited, "satisfactory" solution. What they do instead is to make small incremental changes, constantly monitoring the results of successive decisions, in order to avoid negative consequences. They do not tie this "muddling through" process, however, to policy or goals. They only consider alternatives similar to the present state of affairs. Such a process provides little foundation for the principal who would engage in strategic planning.

## THE MIXED SCANNING MODEL

This, then, is the dilemma of the principal who would initiate strategic planning: the classical model is useless because it is based upon perfect knowledge of alternatives and their consequences, something the principal will never have. But the alternatives of limited goals and limited choices or of simply muddling through are equally unacceptable. The first ignores both the robust nature of the future and its many faces and possibilities. The second is overly conservative and aimless. By definition these methods effectively negate the entire concept of strategic planning.

Amitai Etzioni has described an alternative that he calls "mixed scanning" (Etzioni, 1967, 1986) or "humble decision making" (Etzioni, 1989). The concept of mixed scanning for purposes of planning and decision-making builds upon the metaphor of scanning by satellites with two lenses: wide and zoom. "Instead of taking a close look at all formations, a prohibitive task, or only at the spots of previous trouble, the wide lenses provide clues as to places to zoom in, looking for details" (1986, p.8).

The process he describes is not new; in fact, physicians have used it for years in treating their patients. Doctors start out with a clear, though very general, objective: they want to bring healing to their patients. They also have a good general background of training and experience that tells them on which part of the human body to focus. Since their patients want relief as soon as possible, doctors do not wait for perfect knowledge. On the other hand, they don't commit themselves to an irreversible preliminary diagnosis. After surveying the general health of the patient, they focus on the particular complaint and prescribe a temporary treatment. If it fails, they try something else (Etzioni, 1989).

The term "humble decision making" that Etzioni applies to the mixed scanning model is an interesting one. The model is "humble" because it makes no claim of perfect knowledge, nor does it describe a flawless process. Yet, unlike the incrementalist model, which seeks only alternative adjustments of current process to avoid negative consequences, it is founded upon the fundamental choices about an organization's basic policy and direction. From this foundation it proceeds, in an imperfect yet guided process, to pursue the chosen direction and to effect organizational policy. Etzioni (1989) describes some of the principles of the mixed scanning process.

*Focused trial and error* enables the organization to adapt productively to the reality of partial knowledge. There are two parts to it: (1) "knowing where to start the search for an effective intervention" and (2) "checking outcomes at intervals to adjust and modify the intervention" (Etzioni, 1989, p. 125). The process assumes that there is important information that the executive does not have; but the executive does not pursue this information randomly. Knowledge gained through training and other experience guides the search's start. The principal develops a course of action, in spite of imperfect knowledge, through an adaptive strategy guided by policy.

*Tentativeness*, a commitment to revise the original course when it becomes necessary, is an important piece of this adaptive strategy. Physicians ask their patients to report if symptoms worsen, and they check on their patients after a set period of time to determine if the prescription needs to be continued, stopped, or replaced with something else. Their self-esteem and reputation are not staked on an initial diagnosis and prescription, but on a process that moves logically in pursuit of their overall objective—to make the patient well. Schools also would benefit if they viewed the changes they make—for example, adjustments in curriculum, schedules, or student placements—as tentative and experimental, taking initial action to respond to a problem but waiting to make a final decision until they see the effects of their preliminary adjustments.

*Procrastination* is another element of the mixed scanning strategy. Unlike the immediate decisions that must be made on a daily basis by the principal, strategic decisions are rarely impaired if they are intentionally postponed for a week or a month to pursue more knowledge or wait for improved conditions. *Decision staggering* is one way of procrastinating. Decisions do not have to be all or nothing. We might, for example, begin academic teaming in a middle school with only one grade rather than with all grades at once. Procrastination may also be achieved through *fractionalizing*. We might attempt an experimental curriculum program for only part of a year. Like the farmer who chooses to use a new hybrid seed on only forty acres, we may experiment on a small, safe scale to find out what works and what doesn't work.

*Hedging bets* and *maintaining strategic reserves* are two related adaptive principles. In an uncertain world it is not a good practice to invest all of the organization's resources in an exciting but unproven program, no matter how good it looks. The chance for a revolutionary breakthrough may be lost, but the history of educational innovation suggests that it is better to err on the side of caution and to save resources for investment in programs that show local evidence of success.

Finally, when perfect knowledge is impossible, it is important to make *reversible decisions*. The promise of the "open school" led many communities to construct schools without internal walls to separate classrooms, decisions that were expensive and virtually impossible to reverse totally. Smaller, reversible decisions, guided by overall policy and goals, can be more readily supplemented by other smaller decisions if experience proves them worthwhile.

## PREPARING FOR STRATEGIC PLANNING: SOME BEGINNING QUESTIONS

First and foremost, the mixed scanning model needs a focus, guided by the basic policy and direction of the school: the vision of the school. It has become fashionable for schools to formulate visions and to publicize and celebrate them. One problem, briefly referred to earlier, is that many current school visions simply are not visionary. A vision, properly conceived, should give direction to everything that happens in the school. It should be the basis for all school policies and for the procedures that are developed to support those policies.

One traditional, yet potentially dynamic, way to start on a vision is with the question: "What is the purpose of the school in a democratic society?" Whatever else the answer to this question may include, it must include something about benefit to the student and benefit to the society in which students will spend the rest of their lives. From these two foundations flow particulars about the knowledge, skills, and attitudes that our current and future society will require of students if they are to be personally healthy and socially productive.

Once this has been done on a tentative basis, the principal and colleagues are ready to get their first sense of the scope of the job in front of them. Typically, schools take too narrow a view of the goals of education. To hear many educators (at nearly any level of schooling) talk, their sole purpose is to prepare students for the next level of schooling. It *is* important for the kindergarten teacher to prepare her students for first grade; it *is* important for the middle school to prepare its students for high school; it *is* legitimate for the high school principal to speak of how many of his graduates matriculated into postsecondary institutions. However, there are other more fundamental issues that need to be raised if the vision is to adequately encompass the mission of the school in a democratic society.

A useful question to start with might be: "If nothing is changed from the way it is now, what will our students be doing and how fulfilling will their lives be 10 years from now? Twenty years from now? Twenty-five years?" Obviously, this question needs to be adjusted for the level of school at which the question is asked, but the question does need to be asked in several different time frames. The shorter time frame question may be fairly easy, particularly if it is asked at the elementary school level. Many of the current students are likely to either still be in the public school system or in the early years of postsecondary education. Many of the principal's planning colleagues will have been around for enough years to know where their former students are and how well they are doing. For the longer time periods, information will be less complete but probably sufficient to give a beginning picture. In some settings, this questioning may bring the stark realization that, if nothing is changed, large numbers of the school's current students will be in prison, on welfare, or in menial jobs. In other settings, it may require school professionals to recognize that even their former students in prestigious professional positions are often trapped in dysfunctional habits, unhappy families, shallow social lives, and unfulfilling job situations.

When this first question has been tentatively answered, it is time to ask a second question: "What can we do in our school program to produce a more desirable outcome?" This is a very broad question that also should be answered in only tentative terms at this point. What the question should do is to begin to focus both the task that school professionals face and the additional information that they need to answer it. But before this question is fully answered, two more questions need to be asked: "What changes in society will affect what is expected of our students in the future?" and "What implications do these changes have for how we educate our students?" These questions add further to the complexity of the planning problem and point out even greater gaps in knowledge. The admitted inability of many of the school's stakeholders to answer these questions emphasizes the scope of the task. This is a good time for the principal to introduce a "humble decision making" approach.

## A FRAMEWORK FOR STRATEGIC PLANNING

Etzioni (1986) has outlined a procedure for operationalizing the mixed scanning model. Adapting his guidelines for schools, we describe here what we feel is a reasonable procedure for principals to use with their schools. First, we recommend that on "strategic occasions" the principal bring together the entire school faculty and other selected stakeholders to consider alternative courses of action. Strategic occasions are those that require a major planning initiative by the school. How often they should be is hard to say. As noted below, much will depend on how long it takes to implement ongoing plans and on major changes in the school's environment.

Ordinarily such occasions would occur every few years, though turbulent times may dictate that they occur more often.

The first step in the process is to *list all alternatives* that the principal, the faculty, other stakeholders, and, perhaps, external advisers or consultants, advocate for making the school responsive to the needs that have been identified. (In true brainstorming fashion, no alternatives should be rejected at this point, even if they are not considered feasible.) After examining the alternatives, the group should *remove those to which there are "crippling objections."* Crippling objections may be (1) on utilitarian grounds that required means are not available, (2) on normative grounds that the alternative violates basic values of the school, or (3) on political grounds that the alternative violates the basic values of external persons and groups whose support is necessary. The group should then compare and combine alternatives, and *select a single course of action.* In this winnowing process, lesser objections (not necessarily crippling) will play a part in eliminating some of the options. In order to narrow the alternatives to a single course of action, the group may need to seek out further information and postpone their choice until that information can be considered.

*Before implementing the plan* several other preliminary steps should be taken:

+ break the implementation process into sequential steps;

+ identify the allocation of resources (including the time and energy of individuals and groups) so that the various stakeholders can see what their commitments will be;

+ maintain a strategic reserve of resources to overcome unforeseen difficulties or make adjustments in the implementation process;

+ postpone, to the degree possible, costly and less reversible decisions until later in the process, when increased information on the workability of the process will be available;

+ schedule the collection and processing of additional information (with a somewhat wider scanning lens) so that it will be available at key points to serve subsequent decisions, always assuming that there will be delays in the availability of this information.

*Continue to review the plan while implementing it.* Here the scanning lens should be focused at what Etzioni calls a "semiencompassing" (1986, p. 9) level. Principals should implement this mid-level scanning, a broad look at what is working and what is not, after initiating the first stage of the plan. If the plan is working, they should continue this periodic mid-level monitoring, stretching the scanning intervals until they coincide with scheduled "strategic occasions." Wider scanning should also be performed when implementation runs into difficulties. Wide scanning for a full review should be continued at set intervals even if everything appears to be going right because (a) a previously unseen danger may become more visible, (b) a better strategy may become more apparent and possible, and (c) the original goals may be fully implemented and additional goals may now be considered.

*A plan should be developed for allocating resources (including time and energy) among the various levels of scanning.* Resources should be assigned to:

- normal routines (when plans seem to be proceeding without difficulty);
- semiencompassing reviews of plans;
- overall reviews of plans;
- initial reviews when a whole new problem or strategy is considered;
- more encompassing reviews at set intervals (beyond review of specific plans and before a crisis develops);
- occasional review of these allocation rules.

## BUILDING A STRATEGIC PLAN

Strategic planning is not usually something that principals do. In fact, most principals seldom do planning beyond a single academic year. There seem to be two major reasons for this: (1) Principals are extremely busy; insofar as they have time for planning at all, they plan for the next day, the next month, and, in some cases, for the next school year. (2) Principals are mid-management, and, since schools usually do not have independent fiscal or legal authority, there are many things involved in strategic planning over which they have no control.

Though these concerns have some merit, they don't negate the importance of strategic planning for the school. Effective principals have always been strategic planners. Those who operate completely within the guidelines provided by their school district or state, instead of planning on their own, settle for a truncated vision for their schools. The vision of the effective school encompasses the whole child, as a person and a problem solver, today in school and tomorrow in the larger society. Totally apart from state and district mandates and regulations, the school has a responsibility to build such a vision around its own students, its own staff, and the community that supports it. Such collaborative vision building is more possible because of current trends towards site-based management, and more imperative because of the increasing importance of educating healthy and socially productive citizens for our democratic society.

Using the guidelines proposed by Etzioni (1986), what follows is a general map for the principal who would like to build an effective strategic plan for the school. Times and dates suggested are tentative and should be adjusted to fit the requirements of the particular school. However, enough time should be provided for Stages I and II (laying the foundation and initiating strategic planning) to allow them to reach their full potential for obtaining and processing information. They should not be rushed. Similarly, specific procedures are described and some forms are provided to assist the principal in carrying out strategic planning. These should be modified, as necessary, to fit the particular conditions and needs of a school.

## STAGE I: PREPARING FOR STRATEGIC PLANNING

Although Etzioni (1986) identifies the listing of "all alternatives" as the first step in the strategic planning process, we would recommend that, in order to perform this step adequately, most schools will need to take special steps to prepare for it. Alternatives that are considered will, without preparation, primarily be those that are approximations to what is being done, representing incremental improvements at best. It is likely that school personnel will be bound by the narrow institutional expectations of test scores and other limited criteria, and will ignore the underlying purposes of the schools. If alternatives are to be responsive to a genuine vision for the school, that vision must first be developed. The first stage in building a strategic plan is to get school professionals and other stakeholders to think strategically.

All faculty and key representatives of other stakeholder groups should be included at this stage. Two obvious stakeholder groups are students and parents. Young children probably cannot participate fully in the process, but secondary students can and should be included. In selecting representatives of parents and students, care should be taken to include differing points of view. The purpose of including these groups at this stage is to maximize the valid information that is available for the planning process. To limit participation to those parents and students who always agree with the school professionals will not be productive. At the same time, divergence is not sought for divergence' sake. Representatives should be sought who take a responsible position and are willing to let their ideas grow as they interact with others in the planning process.

Other persons outside the faculty should be added to the planning group based on the same principle of maximizing valid information. Representatives of the community or central office should be added if they are likely to expand the information that is focused on in the planning process.

This stage can be initiated by a series of questions that are proposed to the faculty and other members of the planning group at intervals of approximately two weeks. As suggested earlier, we would propose that the first question be: *"What is the purpose of education in a democratic society?"* After this question has been provided to all members, and before the group comes together to consider it (in about two weeks), the principal should do everything possible to encourage fertile, informal dialogue on the question. When the group comes together, they should review the different answers that have been proposed to this question, tentatively grouping answers that seem to be linked. Enough time needs to be provided for this (at least two hours) to allow all major proposed answers to this question to be expressed and to allow participants to see dominant strands in their collective thinking. It is not necessary to come to consensus or to come up with a single, tight answer regarding the purpose of the school. What is important is that the faculty and others can begin to see where the planning is going.

The principal (and others who are working with the principal as coordinators of the process) should welcome considerable divergence at this point in the process, but they should be careful to push for answers that speak to genuine benefits for their students and/or for society. For instance, if someone suggests that all students be able to read at a certain level, this is not a wrong answer, but it should be treated as an incomplete answer that needs to be explored more fully. This can usually be done through asking the question, "Why?" Reasons provided for the attainment of reading proficiency might include the following: "so they can participate fully in a literate society," "so they can get and hold a decent job," "so that they can function as independent, lifelong learners," "so that they can fully enjoy the human richness that has been captured in literature." All these are excellent answers, and there are probably many others that could be added. What's important is that the focus is on the ends of education, not the means by which it is carried out. This becomes very important for subsequent stages in the strategic planning process.

Immediately following this meeting, the initial planning group should be given the next question: *"If nothing is changed from the way it is now, what will our students be doing and how fulfilling will their lives be 10 years from now? Twenty years from now? Twenty-five years from now?"* Once again, a period of 2 weeks should be provided to allow fertile dialogue to develop around this question. The meeting that focuses on this question should be handled in essentially the same way as the first meeting, allowing divergent opinions to be expressed and allowing an unstated consensus to emerge as all ideas are expressed. Once again, the purpose is to maximize the group's knowledge, including the awareness of positions that are held by different members of the group. The final questions in the preparation stage of the strategic planning process (*"What changes in society will change what is expected of our students in the future?" "What implications do these changes have for how we educate our students?"*) are presented and handled at a third meeting in essentially the same way as the first two questions.

## STAGE II: SELECTING A PLAN OF ACTION

This stage of planning has two major steps: (1) generating alternatives and (2) selecting a single plan of action. The first step is similar to Stage I in that it seeks to maximize valid information, but the second step requires the group to compare different alternatives and make critical choices among them. Thus, while the first step could use the large group format used in Stage I, the second step requires a smaller work group. To enhance the work of the group, it is probably best to use the same group for the entire stage. For these reasons, unless the school is very small, the principal should probably use a smaller group for all of Stage II.

Two cautions, however, must be made. The group should be made up of critical thinkers who, as a group, are representative of the group used in Stage I. This planning group must be seen as credible by the members of the Stage I group in regard to its ability to interpret Stage I and to carry forth the sense of Stage I into subsequent planning. In addition, some regular mechanism must be constructed for the smaller planning group to report back to and get feedback from the original larger group. This can be done through individual contacts, small group meetings, and an occasional total group meeting. Whatever strategy is used, care must be taken to ensure that both the form and the substance of Stage II planning are seen as consistent with Stage I.

Stage II planners should prepare themselves for their work by reviewing the outcomes of Stage I individually and in small, informal groups. Following such preparation, they should meet in a retreat setting away from the school site and, if possible, for more than one day. At this meeting their task will be fivefold: (1) list all alternatives, (2) remove those to which there are crippling objections, (3) combine complementary alternatives when possible, (4) compare the remaining alternatives, and (5) select a single course of action. A checklist for this group process is provided in Figure 3.1.

---

### Figure 3.1. Selecting a Plan of Action for the School

1.  On a separate paper, chalkboard, or transparency, list all alternatives for action that are suggested for the group.

2.  Identify all alternatives to which there are one or more crippling objections. An objection may be crippling for any of several reasons:
    a.  The means to carry it out are not available. (This may refer to inadequate funds, personnel, time, legal basis, or any other necessary resource.)
    b.  It violates the basic values of the school.
    c.  It brings the school into conflict with external groups whose support will be necessary to carry it out.

    Delete alternatives with crippling objections from list of alternatives.

3.  Combine alternatives that are complementary to each other and can be efficiently combined in a single course of action.

4.  Compare alternatives in terms of the following criteria:
    a.  Anticipated benefits.
    b.  Anticipated costs.
    c.  Anticipated disruption to present operations. (Can the alternative be implemented within the present mode of operation? Will it be conducted in addition to the present mode of operation? Will it replace the present mode of operation?)
    d.  Projected time required for full implementation.

5.  Select and refine a single course of action.

---

## Stage III: Planning for Implementation

After selecting an alternative, the same group should make specific plans for implementation. The group may be augmented at this point if additional expertise is needed. We will illustrate how this preimplementation planning might be done with a hypothetical example.

Wilson High School has gone through the first two stages required for strategic planning. The total faculty, together with key parent and student representatives, spent nearly three months preparing themselves for the strategic planning process, thoughtfully considering the likely futures for their dominantly poor and minority student body and comparing these with what they considered to be the purposes of education. Because of the large size of the faculty (approximately 150 persons), it was not feasible for them to conduct most of their Stage I business in a single meeting. They overcame this difficulty by doing much of their work in department groups before convening as a total group. They arrived at the following statement of their collective vision for their school.

*Wilson High School will develop in all its students the skills, knowledge, and attitudes necessary for success and productivity in a rapidly changing world. All students will acquire the linguistic, mathematical, technological, interpersonal, and critical thinking skills necessary to function effectively in a wide range of jobs, many of which have not yet been created. All students will develop a comprehensive knowledge of science, history, and current events that will prepare them for significant roles in all spheres of human endeavor. All students will develop attitudes of caring and responsibility that give them purpose and direction for their lives.*

At a two-day retreat, a smaller planning group (made up of the principal, one assistant principal, two counselors, all department chairs, six other selected teachers, two students, and two parents) arrived at a desired course of action summarized in the following statement:

*Within the next three years Wilson High School will create and implement an educational program that develops independent, flexible learners by infusing critical thinking and problem solving into all aspects of the curriculum. Toward this end the present program will be assessed in terms of what is being done to foster critical thinking and problem solving skills, information will be gathered about exemplary programs throughout the state and nation, professional development will be provided for faculty and staff, and necessary changes will be made in the curriculum.*

After developing this statement, the planners presented it to the larger group, taking care to explain why this particular course of action was selected. The smaller planning group briefly described the major alternatives they had considered and explained that they decided on this course because they felt that critical thinking and problem solving skills fostered all parts of their vision and that they could realistically foster them within the limits of the school's human and material resources. They explained that other programs in support of the school's vision could readily be built upon the foundation that would be developed through critical thinking and problem solving. They also promised to the larger group that they would come back to them for validation of their efforts at regular intervals and that they would keep them abreast of their ongoing work. After obtaining endorsement from the larger group, the planners set about to make more specific plans for implementation. Their overall plan is summarized in Figure 3.2 (pages 53–54).

Note how the plan summarized in Figure 3.2 responds to Etzioni's requirements for preimplementation planning: (1) the process is broken into sequential steps, showing when each piece would be implemented, terminated, or renewed; (2) time, energy, and financial requirements are clearly implied by the delineation of activities; (3) by placing information gathering up front and major changes on the back end of the implementation sequence, the plan holds considerable resources for special allocations during the early months and defers larger, irreversible expenses until a later point when the new program has demonstrated its worth; and (4) the plan makes clear at what points additional information will be needed to make supplementary decisions. While a summary chart like the one displayed in Figure 3.2 does not include all the essential products of Stage III of the strategic planning process, it is an invaluable tool for organizing the work of a planning group and reporting its work to larger audiences.

## STAGE IV: SCANNING DURING IMPLEMENTATION

In addition to the information that is collected to serve key decision points as indicated in Figure 3.2, a "semiencompassing" level of scanning needs to be performed near the end of

## FIGURE 3.2. WILSON HIGH SCHOOL IMPLEMENTATION PLAN

| | Year 1 | Year 2 | Year 3 |
|---|---|---|---|
| | * | | * |
| | JFMAMJJASOND | JFMAMJJASOND | JFMAMJJASOND |

**Assess Current Program**

a. Assess faculty understanding of critical thinking and problem solving and how they can be developed in the high school.

b. Assess the degree to which critical thinking and problem solving are currently being developed at Wilson High School.

c. Formally reassess faculty/staff support at the end of third year.

| | Year 1 | Year 2 | Year 3 |
|---|---|---|---|
| | * | * | |
| | JFMAMJJASOND | JFMAMJJASOND | JFMAMJJASOND |

**Gather Data on Programs in Other High Schools**

a. Search literature.

b. Contact National Association of Secondary School Principals and Association for Supervision and Curriculum Development.

c. Consider implications of work of Coalition of Essential Schools, Paidea Program, and other secondary school reform initiatives.

* **Point at which additional information is needed to serve decision-making.**

| | Year 1 | Year 2 | Year 3 |
|---|---|---|---|
| | * | * * | * |
| **Professional Development** | JFMAMJJASOND | JFMAMJJASOND | JFMAMJJASOND |

a. Teachers will be paid to attend a two-week summer training institute during each of the first two years.

b. Professional development will be held for faculty and staff at monthly meetings during the second academic year.

c. Internal and external consultant help will be made available as the school seeks to implement the new program.

| | Year 1 | Year 2 | Year 3 |
|---|---|---|---|
| | | * | * |
| **Curriculum Changes** | JFMAMJJASOND | JFMAMJJASOND | JFMAMJJASOND |

a. Select four teachers, in different subject areas, during Spring semester of Year 1, to pilot a prototype program in the Fall semester. Provide extensive support to these four teachers.

b. Expand program to include all freshman classes in English, Social Studies, Mathematics, and Science in Fall of Year 2.

c. Expand program to include entire school, adding one class in each subsequent year.

**\* Point at which additional information is needed to serve decision-making.**

the first stage of implementation. The planning group at Wilson High School did this in January of Year 2. The purpose of this scanning activity was to uncover any difficulties in the overall program that may have been associated with the innovations being implemented, as well as any other unforeseen difficulties not picked up by the specific "zoom" assessments scheduled in the planning reflected in Figure 3.2. Subsequent semiencompassing scanning was scheduled for June of subsequent years until all Wilson students in the school were participating in the program. After that, planning related to the critical thinking/problem solving curriculum was incorporated in overall reviews of the school's activity.

## STAGE V: PLANNING FOR SCANNING

In order to continue to strengthen their strategic planning, the principal and faculty at Wilson High School developed a plan for scanning at various levels.

- ♦ Overall reviews are conducted annually in June by the principal and an overall planning group.
- ♦ Semiencompassing reviews are used to get a broad picture of particular projects that are being implemented in the school. (As in the case of the critical thinking/problem solving initiative, these are conducted by the planners associated with the particular project.)
- ♦ Regular "zoom" views are obtained by teachers, department chairs, and others as they assess their routine activities.
- ♦ Initial reviews (such as that which led to the critical thinking/problem solving curriculum) are conducted when other regular scanning activities indicate the need.
- ♦ As part of the annual overall review, the guidelines for scanning will be reviewed.

Strategic planning establishes the framework for organizational oversight in the school. It establishes the basis for choosing among competing priorities. It provides the space in which mid-range planning and short-range planning will take place. It gives direction and purpose to those subsequent planning activities.

## SOME TOOLS TO SUPPORT LONG-RANGE PLANNING

There are many different tools and techniques that have been proposed to support the long-range planning process as it has been described earlier. Two will be presented in this chapter: (1) a modified Q-Sort Goal Ranking Technique and (2) a Cross-Impact Decision Matrix. These are not the only tools that might be used to support strategic planning, but are examples of those that might be used. The principal may prefer other tools and is encouraged to use them. Or, the two techniques presented here may stimulate the principal to create his or her own. In any case, while these supplementary tools are not necessary parts of the strategic planning process, the principal will probably find it useful to have such tools available to support it.

### A GOAL RANKING TECHNIQUE

A goal ranking technique may be incorporated into the strategic planning process to facilitate the transition between the large group input of Stage I and the selection of a plan of action by a smaller group in Stage II. As we've described the process, the first step in Stage II is the generation of alternatives for school action that are based upon input by the school's professional staff and all other key stakeholders in Stage I. In order to increase the fertility of the smaller group's generation of alternatives and to increase their credibility with the larger group, it is often useful for this group to obtain more specific direction from the Stage I group before it starts on its task. This more specific input may be obtained through a modification of a Q-Sort technique for ranking goals that was proposed by Erlandson (1976), based on the earlier work of Downey (1960). This technique is presented here as one device for closing the gap between the first two stages of the strategic planning process.

In response to all the questions considered by the large group in Stage I, but most particularly in response to the last question ("*What implications do these changes have for how we educate our students?*"), each member of the large group is asked to propose one alternative course of action that the school may pursue in order to more effectively prepare its students for the future. Time (perhaps half an hour) can be set aside at the end of the final large group meeting for each member to propose a single alternative on an index card. Additional alternatives may be added over the next few days by group members who come up with what they feel are better alternatives.

The smaller Stage II group can then look over these alternatives and combine them into a more limited number of coherent alternatives that will be presented back to members of the larger group. There is no set number of alternatives that should be presented, but the numbers should probably not exceed 24. In most cases, the number of distinct alternatives generated will probably be less.

The alternatives are then submitted to the members of the larger group, who are asked to rank them in order of preference. Specific instructions for individually ranking a set of 24 alternatives are given in Figure 3.3. Each group member is asked to select what he or she considers to be the nine most preferable alternatives and the nine that are least preferable. From the nine preferred alternatives, the individual selects what he or she considers to be the four best alternatives. For each of these four alternatives, this person states in one sentence why these four have been selected. Similarly, from the nine least preferred alternatives, four are selected that are considered the weakest options, and a sentence giving the rationale for this ranking is provided. Finally, from each of these groups of four, the individual group member identifies one single best and one single worst alternative.

The smaller group that will drive the Stage II process then aggregates the data that have been furnished, identifying those alternatives that have received the greatest support and the least support from the total group. Reasons for greater and lesser support of particular alternatives is also recorded for future use. The aggregate rankings are then disseminated to the larger group for their information and are used by the smaller group in Stage II to guide their deliberations.

As noted, the directions given in Figure 3.3 are based on a list of 24 alternatives. This number is not important, except as an upper limit, and the process can easily be adjusted down to accommodate a smaller number of alternatives.

## FIGURE 3.3. DIRECTIONS FOR RANKING ALTERNATIVES FOR ACTION

Name_____Date_____

Step 1:   From the accompanying list of 24 action alternatives that have been proposed for our school, select the 9 alternatives which you consider to be the most preferable. List the numerical designators of these 9 alternatives in Column C below.

Step 2:   From the list of 24 action alternatives, select the 9 which you consider to be the least preferable. List the numerical designators of these 9 alternatives in Column B.

Step 3:   List the numerical designators of the remaining 6 alternatives in Column IV at the bottom of the sheet.

Step 4:   Of the 9 alternatives you've listed in Column C, select the 4 you consider to be most preferable and list these in Column D. On the back of this sheet, give a one sentence statement of your reason for preferring each of these alternatives. List the remaining 5 alternatives from Column C in Column V.

Step 5:   Of the 9 alternatives you've listed in Column B, select the 4 you consider to be least preferable and list these in Column A. On the back of this sheet, give a one sentence statement of your reason for giving low priority to each of these alternatives. List the remaining 5 alternatives from Column B in Column III.

Step 6:   Of the 4 alternatives indicated in Column D, select the most preferred one and list it under Column VII. List the remaining 3 alternatives from Column D in Column VI.

Step 7:   Of the 4 alternatives indicated in Column A, select the least preferred one and list it under Column I. List the remaining 3 alternatives from Column A in Column II.

Least Preferred <-------------------------------------------------------------->Most Preferred

## A CROSS-IMPACT DECISION MATRIX

A cross-impact decision matrix (Erlandson, 1976) can serve the strategic planning process by forcing the principal and other members of the school's planning group to consider how the school's decisions, represented by its various goals, programs, and initiatives are impacting each other. The value of such a matrix is that schools and other organizations frequently make decisions that conflict with each other and establish programs that actually operate against each other. This phenomenon in organizations has been described and illustrated by Cyert and March (1992). Schools, like other organizations, are extremely complex and their leaders typically give sequential attention to separate goals without realizing that there is a conflict.

A few simple examples from schools should illustrate the point. Once recognizing the problem, principals will be able to generate other similar examples. Consider, for instance, the tremendous (and justified) emphasis that schools put on regular attendance. Most principals are aware of one or more cases where a child's (and perhaps a parent's or a teacher's) desire for "perfect attendance" has brought a sick child to school, jeopardizing the health not only of that one child but of many other children. Most secondary principals are aware of situations where the expectations and requirements of a zealous teacher in one subject area have negative consequences for student performance in other areas. In the early 1980s the state of Texas passed HB 72, an omnibus education bill that among other things contained a provision known as the "no pass, no play" policy. High school teachers and principals in Texas reported that many borderline academic students who became ineligible for athletic participation simply lost all interest in performing academically and, in many cases, dropped out of school altogether. While this particular provision of the law received the greatest attention for its impact on athletics, it also applied to other extracurricular areas. In one case a girl who received a failing grade in Spanish was barred from participation in the school's Spanish club.

New programs often create conflicting pulls on limited resources. Of all the resources the school has, time is probably the most scarce. Anytime a new program or project is considered, planners should think about the time and energy it will take. There are only twenty-four hours in a day, and conscientious principals and teachers generally use them quite judicially. If a new program will take an additional hour per day or three hours a week, what must be given up to accommodate it? Is the new program worth it?

Similar questions must be asked about other resources. Equipment, materials, and supplies are not infinite and must be considered when any new program is considered. Fortunately, they are more typically measured in dollar amounts and therefore are more likely to be taken into account than time. Space, particularly building space, is another finite resource that must be protected. While generally more visible than time, many schools fail to consider it and subsequently find themselves in space and traffic conflicts of their own making.

The cross-impact decision matrix (see Fig. 3.4) can assist the principal and the school's planning group in considering the impact of new initiatives upon each other and upon existing programs. Using the matrix forces planners to consider whether the school's various programs support, conflict with (in terms of goals or claims on resources), or duplicate each other. Such consideration serves decisions by giving information about whether existing or anticipated programs need to be enhanced, curtailed, or otherwise modified.

In some cases, the decision matrix may reveal that separate programs are mutually supportive and may actually provide resources for each other. For instance, a school's community service program may not only establish a valuable bond with the community and provide service opportunities for students but may enhance various academic programs by providing learning resources not available within the walls of the school. These supportive links between programs should be sought out and built into the school's decisions and programs. Rather than competing for a finite group of resources, such decisions can actually build new resources. In the same way, conflicts and duplications between programs can also be revealed.

# FIGURE 3.4. DECISION MATRIX WORKSHEET

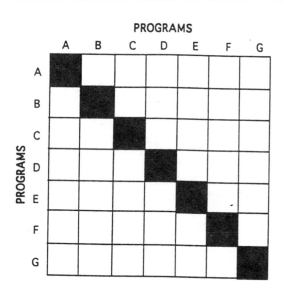

**Directions:** Use the following symbols to indicate how each program affects every other program (columns acting upon rows).

S - Supports

C - Conflicts

D - Duplication of Resources

? - Uncertain

O - No Relation

The cross-impact matrix can be used by the principal and the school's planning group whenever a program is being considered and formulated. For example, it can be used to anticipate the impact of alternative plans of action on current programs during Stage II of the strategic planning process. It can also be used on an annual basis to review the cross-impact of all the school's programs on each other.

We should caution that the decision matrix is not a quick fix or a magical wand that will solve all problems of goal conflict. Because schools are complex organizations, some goal conflict is probably inevitable. However, the principal should find it useful as a strategy for visualizing many potential conflicts and minimizing their negative effects.

## LINKING THE Q-SORT TECHNIQUE AND THE DECISION MATRIX

As we have attempted to emphasize in this document, strategic planning should be a seamless web that links goal formation, setting priorities among goals, and implementation. Without such linkage, a thorough goal setting and prioritization process may have little impact on what happens in the school. We will illustrate this with a fictional example.

Through a comprehensive goal setting process involving its various stakeholders, Washington Elementary School had established the following 12 goals to guide its educational program:

- Develop student understanding and appreciation of other people.
- Develop student appreciation of art and music.
- Develop student pride and feeling of self-worth.
- Develop student language communication skills.
- Develop moral standards of behavior in students.
- Prepare students to assume productive roles in society.
- Develop student health habits.
- Develop student skills in mathematics.
- Develop lifelong learning skills of students.
- Develop student understanding of and ability to apply knowledge from the natural and physical sciences.

+ Develop student understanding of and ability to apply knowledge from history, geography, and the social sciences.

+ Prepare students to be citizens in a democracy.

The Q-Sort technique that we have described chiefly as a device for weighing new alternatives for action can also be used as an effective device for ranking established goals. Washington Elementary School used it for this purpose. Since there were only 12 goals established for the school, a variation of the procedure described in Figure 3.3 was used. (Note: similar variations should be used to adjust for different numbers of goals.) In this case, the six most preferred goals were first chosen by each individual. From these the three most highly preferred were chosen. Of these, the single most preferred goal was selected. A similar procedure was applied to those six goals that, on a comparative basis at least, were least preferred. Individual rankings of representative stakeholders were arranged according to the following pattern:

| I | II | III | IV | V | VI |
|---|----|-----|----|----|----|
| — | — | — | — | — | — |
| | — | — | — | — | |
| | | — | — | | |

Most Preferred_____Least Preferred

Following the rankings of individual stakeholders, four person groups were formed, each representing as much role diversity as possible (e.g., teachers, parents, administrators, community members). These small groups used their individual rankings to develop consensus rankings for their groups. Then the rankings of the small groups were brought together to form the following overall goal ranking for Washington Elementary School.

I  A  Develop student language communication skills.
II  B  Develop student skill in mathematics.
    C  Develop student understanding and appreciation of other people.
III  D  Develop student pride and feeling of self-worth.

      E   Prepare students to assume productive roles in society.

      F   Develop moral standards of behavior in students.

IV  G   Develop student appreciation of art and music.

      H   Develop student understanding of and ability to apply knowledge from history, geography, and the social sciences.

      I   Develop student understanding of and ability to apply knowledge from the natural and physical sciences.

V  J   Develop lifelong learning skills of students.

      K   Prepare students to be citizens in a democracy.

VI  L   Develop student health habits.

In considering these overall rankings, note that no priority was assigned within a roman numeral category (e.g., no difference in preference is shown between Goal B and Goal C). These prioritized goals were then arranged on the Decision Matrix as shown in Figure 3.5 (see pages 66–67).

The Decision Matrix is interpreted as showing how the goals designated in the columns impact the goal designated for each of the rows. Thus, we start at the top with Goal A and go across the cells formed by its intersection with each column to consider how the current and proposed educational programs and activities that are in support of each of the other goals impact upon the attainment of Goal A. We then repeat this process for each of the rows.

To accomplish this process effectively the principal and leadership team at Washington Elementary School first identified the programs that supported their various educational goals. This process, when implemented, helped the leadership team review their programs and activities. If a program or activity could not be seen as supporting one or more school goals, the team scrutinized it carefully to determine if it should be maintained in its present form. As a result of this examination, the team simply dropped several activities that had been maintained for years.

Once this program identification process has been accomplished, teams can consider impacts. As noted earlier, resources of time, energy, space, and money are limited. If an hour of a student's time is used for music instruction, it cannot be used for reading instruction. On the other hand, involvement in a music program may increase the student's sense of pride and involvement in the school program and thereby energize the student for better learning. These are not simple judgments, and the Decision Matrix does not provide a simple way of making them, but it does point to the need for these judgments and helps clarify the points at which they must be made.

We will consider some of the different ways, in our fictional example, in which the leadership team discovered that activities in support of one goal impacted other goals. For example, looking across the row associated with Goal A (develop student language communication skills), the leadership team found that programs supporting several of the other goals limit the amount of time that is provided for reading instruction. Noting these conflicts, the team initiated steps to incorporate reading instruction in other subjects. And, in looking across the row for Goal D (develop student pride and feeling of self-worth), the team determined that certain elements of the mathematics program currently in operation (and in support of Goal B) were having a negative impact on students' pride and sense of self-worth. This case is particularly interesting since, in Row B, school activities designed to promote student pride and self-worth (Column D) were considered to be supportive of mathematics achievement. These two cases involving Goals B and D indicate why it is important to review the row for every goal: goals do not always have equivalent effects on each other.

In the process of considering cross-impact, relative goal priorities are important in determining what actions should be taken. However, this is not a simple process either. All 12 goals identified by Washington Elementary School were considered important or they would not have been included among the school's priorities. In case of conflict, a higher ranked goal shouldn't automatically take precedence over a lower ranked goal. As we noted, rather than diminishing instruction in science, the leadership team took steps to incorporate reading instruction into science. Rather than continuing with the current mathematics program, the team made adjustments so that the program would not impact negatively on student pride and sense of self-worth.

Using goal ranking and cross-impact matrix processes greatly facilitates strategic planning. Goal ranking helps estab-

## FIGURE 3.5. DECISION MATRIX: WASHINGTON ELEMENTARY SCHOOL

| | I | II | |
| --- | :---: | :---: | :---: |
| | A | B | C |
| **I-A** <br> Develop language communication skills of students. | | | |
| **II-B** <br> Develop student skill in mathematics. | | | |
| **C** <br> Develop student understanding and appreciation of other people. | | | |
| **III-D** <br> Develop student pride and feeling of self worth. | | | |
| **E** <br> Prepare students to assume productive roles in society. | | | |
| **F** <br> Develop moral standards of behavior in students. | | | |
| **IV-G** <br> Develop student appreciation of art and music. | | | |
| **H** <br> Develop stdnt. undstndng. & ability to apply knwldg. from hist., geog., & soc. sciences | | | |
| **I** <br> Develop stdnt. undstndng. & ability to apply knwldg. from nat. & phys. sciences. | | | |
| **V-J** <br> Develop lifelong learning skills of students. | | | |
| **K** <br> Prepare students to be citizens in a democracy. | | | |
| **VI-L** <br> Develop student health habits. | | | |

|   | III | | | IV | | V | | VI |
| D | E | F | G | H | I | J | K | L |
|---|---|---|---|---|---|---|---|---|
|   |   |   |   |   |   |   |   |   |
|   |   |   |   |   |   |   |   |   |
|   |   |   |   |   |   |   |   |   |
|   |   |   |   |   |   |   |   |   |
|   |   |   |   |   |   |   |   |   |
|   |   |   |   |   |   |   |   |   |
|   |   |   |   |   |   |   |   |   |
|   |   |   |   |   |   |   |   |   |
|   |   |   |   |   |   |   |   |   |
|   |   |   |   |   |   |   |   |   |
|   |   |   |   |   |   |   |   |   |
|   |   |   |   |   |   |   |   |   |

lish the primary focus of the strategic plan. The cross-impact matrix enables the integration of that focus with all the educational goals of the school. Once established, the cross-impact matrix is a valuable tool for screening the impact of new programs and activities. First, planners should align the new program activity with the goal(s) it serves. Then, they examine horizontally across the appropriate row(s) to see how it is likely to be impacted by other activities. Finally, they trace down the appropriate column(s) to consider how it is likely to impact the attainment of other goals.

The principal should thoughtfully consider the Q-Sort Goal Ranking Technique, the Decision Matrix, and/or other tools in support of strategic planning. Such tools are easy to use and can facilitate the planning process. The two tools presented here have been described in generic form. They will need to be modified to meet the specific needs of a particular situation. The principal is also encouraged to identify and create other techniques that support strategic planning.

## ACTION FOLLOW-UP

Develop an overall strategic plan for an organization of which you are a member.

◆ If you are the head of the organization, present your plan to a group of key stakeholders of the organization and get their feedback for reshaping it, refining it, and putting it into action. Take steps to put the plan into action.

◆ If you are not the head of the organization, present the plan to the head of the organization and explore ways in which this strategic plan, or some modification of it, may be put into action. After the plan has been revised with the collaboration of key stakeholders, put the plan into action.

◆ Make specific plans to use either the Decision Matrix, the Q-Sort Goal Ranking Technique, or some similar tool in the implementation of the strategic plan you have developed. After you have used the tool, modify it to better serve the purposes of your organization.

# 4

# MID-RANGE PLANNING: ORGANIZING THE SCHOOL YEAR

Schools are traditionally organized around a school year, a period that typically begins in late August or early September and continues until late spring. The regular activities of the school and the behaviors of students and staff are built around the school year. Contracts are awarded to school professionals for a school year or for multiples of it. Students commence the school year at a new grade level and, unless something unusual happens, complete that grade level at the end of the school year. Athletic seasons and special events are organized around the school year. Student and teacher assignments, curriculum sequences, and space allocations are all coordinated with each other for efficient delivery of instruction during the period of a school year. The very moods and rhythms of the school reflect the various increments of the school year: "getting off to a good start" in September, the growing excitement before the Christmas break, the unifying experience of a successful football or basketball season, "making it through" to June.

So pervasive is the influence of the school year that many school professionals, including principals, often don't look beyond it. For many principals, "long-range planning" consists of aligning staff, students, textbooks, and space for the coming school year. As we noted in Chapter 3, the development of an educational program that is truly responsive to the needs of all the school's stakeholders requires strategic planning that goes well beyond the school year. Nevertheless, the school year is a critical piece of the American school culture, and the principal who would be successful as an educational leader must learn to organize the school's resources to most efficiently make use of it.

One of the authors, as an elementary school principal, recognizing the symbolic power of the school year as an organizer for the school culture, took special care to emphasize it. She did this most notably through ceremonies at the beginning and the end of the school year.

Each year was opened with a flag raising and lamp lighting ceremony that followed a fairly regular pattern. On the first day of school, everyone (all staff members and all students) gathers around the school flagpole about 30 minutes into the morning to participate in a very formal "raising of the flag" ceremony. As staff and students assemble, the school patrol officers stand in formation, ready to march onto the front yard. The ceremony begins with a trumpet player playing the appropriate "call to colors," and, as the trumpet plays, the patrols march onto the yard and begin to raise the flag. Following the Pledge of Allegiance, the trumpet player plays the Star Spangled Banner. At the end of the national anthem, the patrols march off in formation. Then the principal makes a speech about the expectations for the year, the fun of learning, and similar motivational themes. She then proceeds to light the "lamp of learning" and goes on to explain that each morning the lamp (which will be in her office) will be turned on in order to symbolize for everyone that "we are all learning together."

At the end of the final day of school, everyone once again gathers around the flagpole. Again in a formal ceremony, the patrols march to the flagpole and lead the school in the Pledge of Allegiance. A trumpet player plays the national anthem. This is followed by the "retreat of colors," as the flag is lowered by the patrols. After the flag is lowered, the principal gives a speech about how learning will continue all summer, even though it will not be at the school. She then turns off the "lamp of learning." Staff, students, and parents gives three cheers for the summer and school is formally dismissed.

Now, as a high school principal, she knows that the same ceremonies are not appropriate, but parallel activities can be used. Such activities provide a sense of "beginnings and endings" for staff and students alike. The opening ceremony should create a sense of oneness for everyone when everyone is together for the very first time in the school year. The closing ceremony enables everyone to bring the year to a conclusion.

Within this cultural framework that has been established for the school year, the principal can use a number of fairly standard tools to facilitate planning and the efficient operation of the school organization. There are a number of fairly standard tools that the principal can use in organizing the school year. We will examine three major organizers in depth: the master calendar, the master schedule, and the annual campus plan. We will also briefly present a few of the other instruments that principals may use (handbooks, standard operating procedures, etc.) to strengthen the foundation for organizational oversight.

## THE MASTER CALENDAR

Many things happen in the school year, and there must be some way to prevent conflicts among them. This is a major function of the master calendar. The other function is informational—so that students, teachers, administrators, parents, and others will be informed of what the school is doing so that they can make their plans. Planning for the master calendar begins in the Spring semester prior to the new school year. Everything on the master calendar should be directly correlated with campus planning efforts. Maintaining a master calendar for the year facilitates the following:

+ Plan and scheduling for instruction: staff development, grading periods, testing dates, special curriculum emphases, joint planning for grade levels and/or departments, thematic units, special celebrations (Diez y Seiz, Martin Luther King day, Yom Kippur, American Education week, etc.)

♦ Planning and scheduling for cocurricular activities: spelling bee, bike rodeo, plays, musicals, end-of-unit culminating activities, field days, etc.

♦ Planning and scheduling for extracurricular activities: sports events, club activities, class activities, community activities, etc.

♦ Planning and scheduling for community participation: parent training, P.T.A., neighborhood groups, adult education classes, after-school programs, etc.

The school's master calendar for the year is not totally the prerogative of the school. The schedules and calendars of several bodies outside of the school contain events that the master calendar of the school must include. For example, the school district in which the school operates will have a calendar, usually scheduling holidays, staff development days, and other special events. Most states have set aside special dates for statewide testing. Externally developed athletic schedules set up dates for games and tournaments. The list goes on. The school usually has no control over these, and, consequently, they should be put on the calendar first.

Once these externally mandated dates have been established on the school's master calendar, the principal and the faculty can begin to set their own dates. The first step is to set up times for regular schoolwide meetings: faculty meetings, building leadership team meetings, etc. Then the calendar is given to departments (in secondary schools), grade level groups (in elementary schools), and other functional groups (e.g., the school's counseling staff) to establish other dates on the calendar. After the first draft of the master calendar is completed, the principal and building leadership team should review it for the purpose of identifying and removing direct conflicts (i.e., conflicts due to the use of the same time or space) and indirect conflicts (e.g., scheduling an incompatible activity just before the administration of statewide tests). The master calendar should then be submitted to the entire school staff for review and suggestions for change.

The school calendar must be readily available to everyone in the school who has need of the information on it. It should be posted in the conference room, the teachers' lounge, the principal's office, and any other setting in the school where its information might be used. It needs to be placed where it is visible and available for planning purposes.

The principal and assistant principals should have identical style calendars, which are updated at their regular meetings. These calendars may be structured to include a single year or may cover multiple years so that the principal can look at a glance to see where the school came from and where it's going. Sometimes these calendars are furnished by the school district, with key districtwide dates already printed in them. Or they can often be obtained at no cost through companies that have contracts with the schools (rings, cap and gowns, etc.). Whatever the source, these common calendars enhance the communication between the principal and the assistant principals and serve the principal's quest for a unified school direction and purpose.

Once established it must be remembered that the master calendar is still a planning tool; it must continue to be developed during the course of the school year. The principal and school leadership team should meet on a weekly basis to make additions and modifications to the school calendar. When new knowledge suggests that times and dates, within the control of the school, should be modified, the principal should not hesitate to make these changes. The master calendar should be a living document to direct the school. However, a word of caution should be added here. Since teachers, parents, and many other individuals have set their personal calendars around the school's calendar, care must be taken to ensure that any additions or modifications will not cause significant problems for these school stakeholders.

## THE MASTER SCHEDULE

Perhaps the most graphic planning document at the school district level is the annual budget. Much can be said about a school district's philosophy of education, and often published statements of school district philosophy make global promises of educational good for every student in the school district and for every need in society. However, dollars are limited, and when the school board and the superintendent choose to put more money in one category than in another, they are making a very concrete statement of their true educational philosophy. They may make statements about equality of opportunity for all students but the budget may show that some types of students are clearly favored over others.

Most principals in the United States do not have total control over their budgets—though with site-based management they may be increasingly getting more. However, they do have a lot of control over the allocations of time and space within their buildings. These resources, like dollars, are always limited, and how a school allocates them tells more about educational priorities than all the statements of educational mission and vision that the school can produce. For instance, a high school principal and his or her staff must regularly make a choice between advanced electives with small student enrollments and average class size in nonelective classes. If the principal chooses a large number of advanced electives with small student enrollments, the numbers of students in other classes must increase. Given a constant student enrollment in the school (let's say 1000) and a constant number of teachers in the school (let's say 50), the average number of students per teacher per class will be 20. If an advanced elective enrolls only seven students, the average size of other classes will increase. This may be a wise choice or a foolish choice, depending on the circumstances, but it is a choice that reflects the educational philosophy of the school and its principal. Attempting to match students, faculty, subjects, and classrooms inevitably results in conflicts, as different priorities make claims on the same resources. How these conflicts are resolved should clearly reflect the stated philosophy of the school.

This is where the annual planning of a school is directly linked with the strategic planning described in Chapter 3. The advantage of strategic planning is that it enables the systematic consideration of alternative school options. But unless the priorities identified in strategic planning are translated into the annual plans of the school, they will be of no avail. The master schedule of the school, together with staffing decisions that are made to support it, is the principal concrete manifestation of the school's educational priorities.

## SCHEDULING THE HIGH SCHOOL

Work on the master schedule in a high school actually begins in the Fall semester of the previous year. Two types of data go into this early work: (1) major changes in course offerings and curriculum stimulated by strategic planning, and (2) minor adjustments in course offerings. Generally, new courses for the following school year must be approved by school district officials sometime during the Fall semester. Of course, when major changes in curriculum or class structure emanate from strategic planning, key school district officials should have been brought on board at a much earlier time and, in fact, should have been part of the strategic planning process. Registration of students should begin early in the Spring semester and should be completed by the middle of that semester. Each student should be seen and counseled with individually. Before the school year ends, each student should verify the courses for which he or she has registered. A careful registration process will prevent many problems when the new school year begins and will greatly reduce the number of schedule changes that must be made at that time. The registration process also is a tool to inform the principal about staffing and building space needs so that last minute adjustments may be made.

An example of a timeline for a high school scheduling process is presented in Figure 4.1.

## REVISING THE MASTER SCHEDULE

Although the master schedule is an annual document, it should be the result of long-range planning and clearly tied to strategic objectives. Changes made out of desperation ("because something different needs to be done") or because other schools are doing it are ill conceived. We will follow the case of Edgemont High School, in which the strategic planning process clearly revealed that its present master schedule was not serving the needs of its students. We will follow the school staff through their search for alternatives, examining the pros and cons of several different types of high school schedules in

FIGURE 4.1. EDGEMONT SCHOOL DISTRICT SCHEDULING
PROCESS 1995–1996

| DATE | SCHEDULING PROCESS | PERSON RESPONSIBLE |
|---|---|---|
| November 18 | Principals present their course or program changes to Assistant Superintendent for Instruction. | Principals |
| December 12 | Changes for 1995-96 school year presented to Board. | Assistant Superintendent for Curriculum and Instruction |
| December 14 | Notify Print Shop of major printing due in January. | Assistant Superintendent for Curriculum and Instruction |
| January 13 | Registration booklets and registration forms will be turned in to Print Shop. | Principals & Director of Secondary Education |
| January 20 | Input all courses into Master Schedule from course selection sheets. Verify exact match between registration forms and master schedule. | Principals |
| January 30 | Begin registering students. | Coordinator of Counselors, Counselors, and Principals |
| March 31 | Registration closes. | Coordinator of Counselors, Counselors, and Principals |

| DATE | SCHEDULING PROCESS | PERSON RESPONSIBLE |
|---|---|---|
| April 7 | Registration data entered in computer. | Director of Computer Services |
| April 10 | Tallies and course lists mailed to each campus principal. | Director of Computer Services |
| April 10 | Verification of course lists from first tallies. | Department Heads and Program Supervisors |
| April 10 | Verification of student registration data. | Counselors |
| April 18 | Corrections of first tallies completed. | Principals |
| April 21 | Second tallies mailed to campuses; corrections to be continued. | Director of Computer Services |
| April 28 | Staffing requests and Space needs (portables and/or renovations) to Assistant Superintendent for Curriculum and Instruction and Director of Building and Grounds | Principals |
| April 28 | Student verification sheets sent to 9-12 schools. Available on request to 6-8 schools. | Director of Computer Services |
| May 10 | Master Schedule updated with sections and ready to run loads. | Principals |

| DATE | SCHEDULING PROCESS | PERSON RESPONSIBLE |
|---|---|---|
| May 10 | Principals to send master schedule updates; loads to be run throughout month (upon request). | Principals |
| May 19 | Corrections from verification sheets completed. | Principals |
| May 19 | Notify faculty of their PROBABLE teaching assignment. | Principals |
| June 9 | Re-enrollment list to 8th grade principals. | Director of Computer Services |
| June 9 | Retentions reviewed. | Principals |
| July 28 (PROBABLE) | Summer school ends. | Principals and Counselors |

| DATE | SCHEDULING PROCESS | PERSON RESPONSIBLE |
|---|---|---|
| August 1 | Course changes made for students completing summer courses and failures adjusted. | Principals and Counselors |
| August 1 (Or as soon as Summer School is over) | Review placements/retentions. | Principals |
| August 3 | Final loads completed. Principals sign off at 5% conflict rate or less. | Director of Computer Services, Principals, Director of Secondary Education |
| August 7 | Paper schedules | Director of Computer Services and Principals |
| August 8 | Schedule cards ordered after verification of paper schedules and picked up by principals upon request. | Director of Computer Services |
| August 10-11 | Pass out students' schedules. | Principals and Counselors |

relation to the school's educational values. Although this case is tied to the high school experience, the basic questions and considerations apply at every level of school—elementary school, middle school, or high school.

Based on the school district's statement of philosophy, their own mission statement, and the parameters adopted by the strategic planning team, Edgemont High School set about in the fall of 1993 to consider structural alternatives to its master schedule. With the support and encouragement of the superintendent and the school board, the principal and the Campus Performance Improvement Team (CPIC) began to visit and investigate other high schools that had (successfully or not) restructured the organization of the school day.

A conventional seven-period day had been in operation at Edgemont High School for the past two years, and while it was not popular among the teachers, a group of parents who had originally pressed for its adoption wanted to retain it. The teachers expressed a strong interest in identifying an alternative form of scheduling that would at one time be responsive to the desires of parents and yet provide a course framework that was more pedagogically sound from the viewpoint of the teachers. Initiating an investigation of alternatives was in line with the strategic guideline of "not allowing past practice or fear of change to interfere with the consideration of any new idea."

A restructuring team was chosen by CPIC to begin the basic investigative work. In the 1993–94 school year they began to visit different high schools. The team included parents and community members, in accordance with strategic planning guidelines. After viewing schools with A/B Block Schedules and Accelerated Block Schedules, the team made a recommendation to the principal that those schedules not be pursued due to concerns about the impact of their structures on the delivery of instruction. The chief concern with the A/B Block Schedule (in which students take each class for an extended period of time every other day) was that many students would be too immature to adequately schedule their own time and responsibilities if assignments were not due the next day. The concern with the Accelerated Block Schedule (in which students take classes for longer periods each day over a fewer number of weeks) was that the pace of learning would be too fast, particularly in classes such as foreign languages that require time to fully integrate new sounds, vocabulary, and grammatical structures. Although there was considerable difference of opinion among team members and across the faculty, the team made the recommendation and CPIC confirmed that the high school would remain on the seven-period day for the 1994–95 school year while continuing to search for the right match for the school and community.

In the fall of 1994, a larger restructuring team was formed by CPIC for the purpose of continuing the search. Based on information they had received, the team visited two school districts in the state and two outside the state. The visit to a nearby high school, similar in size and diversity to Edgemont, and the visit to one of the out-of-state schools convinced the team to pursue the trimester plan. A second visit was made to the nearby school by a larger group, which included students as well as staff and parents. The strengths and weaknesses of the trimester plan were examined in depth as the restructuring team sought to reach a conclusion that they could recommend. A summary of these advantages and disadvantages, as listed by the restructuring team, is contained in Figure 4.2 (see pages 82–83). CPIC recommended the trimester plan to the principal, who in turn recommended it to the superintendent and the school board. Approval was given to begin working out the details for the adoption of a trimester schedule.

Many meetings followed. The restructuring team met with the district's curriculum and instruction staff in December and, in January, made a presentation to the whole faculty at Edgemont High School. Later in January a presentation was made to the school board. This was followed by a series of meetings that were held to inform the public. Parents and community members were invited on three different evenings in February to hear the report of the restructuring team. At the March meeting of the school board it was decided to begin the trimester plan in 1996–97 in order to allow time to work on concerns raised about the curriculum and staff development that would be needed to support the trimester plan.

In May of 1995, a committee made up of the principal and other key teachers and administrators, from the central office

## FIGURE 4.2. ADVANTAGES AND DISADVANTAGES OF TRIMESTER SCHEDULING PLAN

### PERCEIVED ADVANTAGES OF TRIMESTER SCHEDULING PLAN
**As Formulated in Committee Meeting on 1/18/95**

1) Second chance
2) Flexibility
3) Longer class periods (closure; labs)
4) Opportunity to take more courses
5) Less stress
6) Reduce failure rate
7) Fewer class changes
8) Forces restructured curriculum
9) Attendance increase
10) Flexibility for working students
11) Teach four classes instead of six
12) Longer planning period
13) More innovative teaching
14) More time to complete lab
15) Course load may be split
16) Increased focus on state competency test
17) Concentrated learning time
18) Bonding time to know students
19) Time to use technology
20) Meets requirements of SBOE
21) More college credit through tech prep
22) Teacher/student rotation
23) No changes in grade reporting
24) Mixed classes (levels)
25) Immediate remediation
26) Easy adjustment from 8th to 9th
27) Later starting time
28) Less bus transportation
29) No finals before Christmas on trimester plan
30) Better addresses learning styles
31) Attendance
32) Senior arena scheduling

## Perceived disadvantages/Questions
## of Trimester Scheduling Plan
## As Formulated in Committee Meeting on 1/18/95

1) More time to schedule
2) More finals
3) Transfer students (to Edgemont)
4) Teachers' failure to adjust
5) Mandatory that teachers adjust
6) More initial work at beginning (teachers)
7) More restriction on individualized curriculum
8) More make-up work per class if absent
9) Five absences each semester
10) Gaps in curriculum
11) Frequent student changes
12) Senior readjustment
13) Singleton class
14) Poor planning/cramming at last minute
15) Staffing needs
16) "Double" electives
17) Restructure 95/96? Or 96/97?
18) Increase class size?
19) Revise curriculum (Staff Development)
20) Negative to AP classes? (Quality/success)
21) Fear of "watered-down" curriculum
22) Technology to restructure
23) Increase paperwork for Spec. Ed.
24) Possible vocational funds (loss)

as well as from the high school, began work on establishing timelines for staff development and curriculum change. This work was completed early in June. This development work proceeded fairly well on schedule throughout most of the 1995–96 school year. At established points in the process, they reported their progress back to the entire faculty. Special meetings were also held each semester to keep parents abreast of progress.

In pursuing the trimester plan, Edgemont High School (and the superintendent and school board of the Edgemont School District) hoped to create a climate in which their overall strategies and goals could be carried out. By including all stakeholders in the planning and discussion of the plan, there were no major upsets or political battles. At every stage persons with expertise and concern were brought into the planning. For instance, the district director of transportation was included so that an analysis could be made of the effect of the trimester plan on the busing schedules for all the schools in the district. The athletic director and his assistant were brought in for a similar reason. What one campus decides to do with its time schedule obviously will have impact throughout the district. What made the process successful at Edgemont was that all stakeholders clearly bought into the vision of the school and by jointly working on the identified problems over a reasonable period of time, avoided negative feelings caused by stress and inadequate information. Other high schools in different locations and with different student populations and problems may disagree with Edgemont High School's decision in favor of the trimester plan. They will find it hard to improve on the process by which the decision was reached.

## A NOTE ON COMPUTER SCHEDULING

The scheduling process for modern high schools has been facilitated tremendously through computer programming. Computer programs to support various types of class schedules are on the market, and programmers are available to write programs for the particular needs of schools or school districts. Each program proclaims its own strengths, and the school person, unfamiliar with the alternatives, can easily be misled.

To find the right program for a particular school requires a thorough investigation by knowledgeable people; many of these programs are being presented by salespeople who do not understand the needs of the school. Buyer beware!

## SCHEDULING AT THE ELEMENTARY SCHOOL

Clearly, scheduling at the elementary school is not nearly so intricate as at the secondary school level. Yet while it is not so complex, it is extremely important. The increased use, by elementary schools, of various professional resources (e.g., special education teachers, reading specialists, ESL support, gifted and talented programs, etc.) have required that elementary principals carefully schedule the time of staff and students and the space in which they operate so that the impact of these resources on the educational process can be maximized. Nevertheless, because, in most elementary schools, a single classroom teacher has primary responsibility for each child, the allocation of personnel time and building space can usually be handled in a developmental manner through standing committees, grade level teams, and resource personnel.

Yet the elementary principal still has the responsibility to see that both personnel and space are effectively and efficiently used. While the elementary schedule can be more flexible and shift almost on a daily basis to meet emerging needs, and while most of this flexibility can be adequately handled by the teachers and other personnel involved, the principal must still oversee the process to ensure that no student's individual needs are being ignored and that teachers and resource personnel are successfully collaborating to focus school resources on those student needs. Effective team development, as described in Chapter 2, and constant attention to the school's mission and vision will go a long way toward ensuring that time, space, and other resources are effectively scheduled in the elementary school.

## THE CAMPUS PLAN

In recent years, considerable emphasis has been placed on campus planning and the development of campus plans. There are at least two major sources that support this emphasis: (1) the general recognition that, in order to be accountable to both their internal and external stakeholders, schools, like other organizations in the public and private sectors, must publicly present their goals and the means by which they intend to achieve them, and (2) the emergence of site-based management and the empowerment of local school stakeholders, including teachers and parents.

The campus plan should be the annual explication of the school's strategic plan. As in the case of the strategic plan, all significant groups of school stakeholders should be included. While the group that puts together the annual campus plan need not be identical with the primary group that shaped the strategic plan (and probably shouldn't be), there should probably be sufficient overlapping membership between the two groups to ensure compatibility and continuity between the two plans.

Campus plans for improvement should look at a number of different things.

- ◆ The results of the school's strategic planning should give principal direction to the annual campus plan.
- ◆ Results from statewide tests.
- ◆ Attendance data.
- ◆ Dropout data.
- ◆ Graduation rates.
- ◆ School climate surveys.
- ◆ SAT/ACT scores of graduating seniors.
- ◆ Locally developed evaluations and needs as-sessments, aimed at specific school needs.

In short, annual campus plans look at many of the same things that are examined by strategic planning, and, in fact, should depend heavily on the strategic plan for direction in gathering data. However, the annual campus plan is more limited in its focus. It looks at what can be accomplished during a single year and focuses on three to five objectives that can reasonably be accomplished during that year. The data that are collected in pursuit of the plan should serve as interim benchmarks for the strategic planning process.

Annual goals are established through a collaborative process during the Spring semester that precedes an academic year. Campus plans for achieving these goals should explicate the strategies that will be used to accomplish them, the person(s) who will be chiefly responsible for each segment, the resources that will be encumbered by the various activities, the dates in which they will occur, and the means by which they will be evaluated. The campus plan should also include strategies for staff development that will be pursued during the year, either to accomplish the annual goals or for over-arching strategic goals in later years. It should also identify strategic staffing needs that must be filled if goals are to be accomplished. Evaluation of goal achievement is done in late spring by the principal and the group or task force that developed it and has been monitoring it. By this time, of course, the campus plan for the next year is well along in its development and can benefit from the lessons learned by this evaluation.

Excerpts from two annual campus plans are provided in Figures 4.3 and 4.4. The reader should keep in mind in viewing them that they are not complete campus plans; they do not review needs assessment, analysis of those needs, or statements of the school's mission, vision, and beliefs. However, they are instructive on how campus plans translate goals into performance objectives, objectives into strategies, and strategies into specific activities.

## OTHER TOOLS FOR ORGANIZING THE SCHOOL YEAR

So far in this chapter on mid-range planning we have examined three organizers for the school year: the master calendar, the master schedule, and the campus plan. A number of other tools are also available to the principal for organizing the school's routines that continue throughout the year. These tools, usually in the form of handbooks or similar documents, cover a wide range of topics: procedures for teachers, procedures for students, information for parents and community members. The specific number of handbooks and other documents that may exist in a school is almost limitless.

*(Text continues on page 96.)*

---

## FIGURE 4.3. CAMPUS IMPROVEMENT PLAN: HAPPY VALLEY ELEMENTARY SCHOOL 1995–1996

---

**GOAL:** All students who leave Happy Valley Elementary School at the end of the fifth grade will have demonstrated competency in the problem solving process in order to become critical thinkers in all subject areas.

**PERFORMANCE OBJECTIVES:**

1. On the May, 1996, administration of the Statewide Competency Test (SCT) a minimum of 70% of eligible third, fourth, and fifth grade students taking the math portion of the SCT will meet or exceed minimum expectations on the math exam.

2. On the May, 1996, administration of the SCT, a minimum of 90% of eligible third, fourth, and fifth grade students taking the reading section of the SCT will meet or exceed minimum expectations on the reading exam.

3. On the May, 1996, administration of the SCT, a minimum of 80% of eligible fourth grade students taking the writing portion of the SCT will meet or exceed minimum expectations on the writing test.

4. The academic achievement of all students will increase in the areas of math, reading, and language arts so that at least 95% of all students are achieving a minimum of 70% mastery in all subject areas each six weeks.

5. The students at Happy Valley Elementary School will attain a minimum of 97% in average daily attendance for the 1994-1995 school year.

**STRATEGIES:**

1. Staff and students will broaden their use of the problem solving process across the curriculum.

2. Students will have increased access to small group instruction.

3. Staff will provide a language enriched environment to accelerate oral language development.

**Campus Improvement Plan: Happy Valley Elementary School**

**1995 - 1996**

STRATEGY I:     Staff and students will broaden their use of the problem solving process across the curriculum.

Activity:       **Staff Development**

A.    In-Service sessions will be held on waiver days, during faculty meetings, or on non duty days.

    Timeline/Dates: August 1995 - May 1996

*   Math Writing
Lisa Martinez, Instructional Guide

*   SCT Test Specs and Test Taking Skills
Elizabeth Benton, Math Representative

*   Problem Solving & Oral Language Development Across the Curriculum
Lisa Martinez, Instructional Guide

*   Math Vocabulary Development
Lisa Martinez, Instructional Guide

*   Math in Field Experiences
Dr. Greta Marcus, Principal

*   Higher Order Questioning Strategies
Dr. Martin Cohen

*   Visual Math
Lisa Martinez, Instructional Guide

B.    Model teaching: Will be done by Elizabeth Benton, Math Representative; Dr. Greta Marcus, Principal; Lisa Martinez, Instructional Guide.

    Timeline/Dates: September 1995 - May 1996

C.    Peer Demonstration: Every teacher will pair with another teacher on campus and teach a problem solving lesson once every six weeks from October 1995 - May 1996 and provide feedback on the lesson observed.

**Campus Improvement Plan:  Happy Valley Elementary School**

**1995 -1996**

D.    Instructional snapshots will be completed in each classroom between September and November 1995 with a follow-up snapshot to be done in each room between March 1996 and May 1996.

Formative Evaluation (August 1995 - May 1996):

Evidence of implementation will be documented by (1) sign in sheets and evaluation sheets from in-service sessions, (2) instructional snapshot record sheets, (3) feedback from peer demonstrations provided each six weeks, and (4) self-assessment folders for evaluation of the staff development activities of the year.

Summative Evaluation (May 1996):

Evidence of implementation of skills learned through staff development will result in increased student performance on the SCT for 3rd, 4th, & 5th grade students and an increased percentage of all students achieving mastery in all subject areas each six weeks.

Resources:  Title I and Local Funds

**Activity:    Participation in the Problem Solving Process**

A.    All students will participate in at least two informal math writing activities each week.  Each teacher will submit one writing sample per month to Dr. Marcus. Samples will be turned in between September 1995 and May 1996.

Responsible Persons:  Academic Coordinating Teachers; Candice Smith, Goal Setting Chair, Instructional Leadership Team (ILT); Dr. Greta Marcus, Principal.

B.    All students, grades 1-5, will do Arithmetic Daily Drill exercises two days a week and Daily Mathematics or the Problem Solver exercises three days a week. Pre-kindergarten and kindergarten students will participate in problem solving activities each day.

Timeline/Dates:  September 1995 - May 1996.

Responsible Persons:  Candice Smith, Elizabeth Benton, Bill Carlson, Dr. Greta Marcus.

**Campus Improvement Plan: Happy Valley Elementary School**

**1995 - 1996**

C.  All campus personnel will utilize SCT math word lists in developing a common campus-wide vocabulary. The lists will be disseminated to all personnel no later than October 1, 1995, and will be utilized through May, 1996.

Responsible Persons: Candice Smith, Goal Setting Chair, ILT; Lena Carini, 4th Grade Teacher.

D.  All students will participate in Calendar Math daily.

Responsible Persons: Candice Smith, Goal Setting Chair, ILT; Lisa Martinez, Curriculum Guide; Bill Carlson, Administrative Assistant.

E.  All staff members will be trained in Visual Math and will implement it in the classroom throughout the year.

Responsible Person: Lisa Martinez, Curriculum Guide.

Formative Evaluation (August 1995 - May 1996):

Math writing samples from each grade level will be shared with Dr. Marcus, Mrs. Martinez, and Mr. Carlson each month. Feedback from Math writing samples will highlight the use of SCT Math vocabulary and the problem solving process. Daily Math and Problem Solver exercises will be reflected in the lesson plans by day and designated time frame. They will be checked each six weeks by Dr. Marcus and Mr. Carlson. Informal walk-throughs will be conducted by Dr. Marcus, Mrs. Martinez, and Mr. Carlson on a monthly basis.

Summative Evaluation (May 1996):

Evidence of the implementation of the activities listed above will be shown by improved SCT scores for all students and an increased percentage of all students achieving mastery in all subject areas each six weeks.

Resources: Title I and Local Funds.

## FIGURE 4.4. CAMPUS IMPROVEMENT PLAN: EDGEMONT HIGH SCHOOL 1995–1996

**I) DISTRICT GOAL:** To improve student achievement and instill self-confidence through high expectations for all students.

**A) Campus Performance Objective:** To increase the average SAT score by 10 points in each area (while maintaining 60% seniors taking) and 2 points on ACT.

| Activities | Person(s) Responsible | Resources | Beginning Date | Ending Date | Evaluation |
|---|---|---|---|---|---|
| 1. Emphasize academic and critical thinking reading skills. | Principal | Money | 10/94 | 5/95 | SAT/ACT data |
| 2. Recognition in newspapers, assemblies, bulletin boards, etc., of academic achievements. | Counselors, administrators, site based team | Time, info to proper places | 9/94 | 5/95 | Number of occurrences |
| 3. Investigate addition of pre-AP courses | Aministrators, counselors, exit level teachers | Training, money | 10/94 | 5/95 | Number of occurrences implemented |
| 4. Continue to pay for PSAT for juniors and honors 10th grade | Principal | Money | 10/94 | 10/94 | Improved SAT scores and numbers taking |
| 5. Investigate addition of another AP class (in addition to 4 currently offered). | Teachers, principal | Training, money | 11/94 | 5/95 | Addition of class |
| 6. Monitor Correlation of grades and test scores | Counselors, principal, teachers | Money | 9/94 | 6/95 | Grades and test scores, data |

-Continued-

**I) DISTRICT GOAL:**

**A) Campus Performance Objective:**

**- CONTINUED FROM PAGE 1 -**

| Activities | Person (s) Responsible | Resources | Beginning Date | Ending Date | Evaluation |
|---|---|---|---|---|---|
| 7. Continue high level academic performance in interscholastic competition. | UIL coaches, administration | Money, time | 11/94 | 3/95 | Performance in interscholastic competition |
| 8. Addition of academic decathlon | Teachers | Money, time | 9/94 | 3/95 | Competing in contest |
| 9. All students to read at least two books per six weeks across the curriculum. Encourage to read from AP list. | Teachers, administrators | Books | 8/94 | 5/95 | Compilation of readings required |
| 10. Develop and use school-based end of course tests | Teachers | Time | 8/94 | 5/95 | Number of tests developed |

I) DISTRICT GOAL: To improve student achievement and instill self-confidence through high expectations for all students.

A) Campus Performance Objective: To increase the average scores on state mandated tenth grade exit test, by 10 points in math, 5 points in reading, and 7 points in writing, while closing the gap between high performing students and minority and educationally disadvantaged students.

| Activities | Person (s) Responsible | Resources | Beginning Date | Ending Date | Evaluation |
|---|---|---|---|---|---|
| 1. Implement plan (attached) of activities to support testing objective | Principal, teachers | Instructional materials (software) related to testing objective | 9/94 | 5/95 | Test scores |
| 2. Monitor teacher lesson plans and tests for compliance | Asst. Principal | Tests, lesson plans | 9/94 | 5/95 | Test scores |
| 3. Closely monitor all at-risk, minority, and low socio-economic students | Counselors, teachers | Grades | 9/94 | 5/95 | Test scores |
| 4. All teachers to be knowledgeable of state testing objectives | Asst. Principal | Lesson plans, tests | 9/94 | 5/95 | Test scores |
| 5. Use study skills, advisement, and content mastery to increase test mastery | Asst. Principal, teachers | Lesson plans | 9/94 | 5/95 | Test Scores |

**I) DISTRICT GOAL:** To attract and retain the highest quality teachers and other employees with emphasis on minorities through competive salaries and benefits.

**A) Campus Performance Objective:** Maintain campus committee, when possible, in recruiting and interviewing.

| Activities | Person (s) Responsible | Resources | Beginning Date | Ending Date | Evaluation |
|---|---|---|---|---|---|
| 1. Provide training for teachers | Principal | Training | 9/94 | 8/95 | Completion of training teacher; evaluation of effectiveness |
| 2. Increase team involvement in hiring. | Principal | Training | 9/94 | 8/95 | Number of teachers recommended by committee |

The purpose of these documents is to enhance communication in the school. As we have seen, much communication flows in the typical school, and there is always a concern about whether important information will reach the intended users in a manner that promotes both comprehension and, ultimately, implementation. Much of this information, particularly what is new and immediate, flows by word of mouth at meetings and on a person-to-person basis, or by one-page bulletins and announcements. These channels are invaluable and are heavily used. In many schools they tend to be overused. Handbooks and brochures, typically reviewed and, if necessary, revised, on an annual basis, can take part of the load off other channels by carrying the critical information of semipermanent policies and guidelines. As we have seen, planning is critical in maintaining direction in the school. Handbooks and similar documents enable all the school's stakeholders to be beneficiaries of this planning. For instance, a new teacher who wants to review how to handle an attendance or a discipline problem can get this information from a handbook without bothering an administrator or another teacher. By reviewing in advance the policy on handling sexual harassment, the principal will not have to waste precious time finding out what to do when a case arises. By having an attractive brochure or prospectus describing the school, the principal will have something valuable to give to new parents that will supplement whatever is communicated orally. Standard documents for these and a host of other uses can add considerably to the efficient operation of the school.

Who produces these documents? In many school districts, the district office will do much of this work for the school: a standard teacher handbook, a uniform discipline policy, a textbook adoption policy. These are of great value to the principal and can save the school considerable time and expense by not having to do its own. However, in many of these areas it is impossible to have policies that cover the requirements and contingencies of a particular school. Where this is the case, we would encourage the principal to make the necessary investment of time and money to provide the school's stakeholders with a document that supplements the material provided by the school district. Such tools are invaluable for communicating the school's message to its stakeholders. For example, what particular policies and procedures call out to teachers, students, or parents: "We are Happy Valley Elementary School or Edgemont High School"? These things should be included in special school documents that supplement the information provided by the district. They are the reflection of campus pride and personality. Often they can be combined in a single document with the district policies. Where there is no district document, the principal may find it necessary to provide all the guidelines and direction through a campus document. This is more work, but it may be necessary.

What specific information is included in these documents? This will vary widely from school to school and from school district to school district, depending on local needs. We will, however, try to give suggestions of the major topics that may be included in various types of handbooks and brochures.

A teacher handbook should probably contain these items:

- A welcome to teachers and a clear affirmation of their importance in the school.
- A statement of the school's vision and mission statements.
- A map of the school.
- The daily schedule of the school.
- The school calendar.
- A roster of faculty, administrators, counselors, clerical staff, and custodial staff, showing duty assignments.
- Expectations of teachers, in regard to shared leadership, instruction, curriculum development, lesson plans, student relations, parent relations, personal appearance and conduct, absences and preparation for substitutes, and professional growth.
- Teacher appraisal policies and procedures.
- Professional development resources and opportunities.
- Teacher committee assignments.

- Regular and special duties (for example, bus dock duty) of teachers.
- Identification of resources and facilities available in the school and the district (workroom, copying facilities, computer assistance, professional library, etc.).
- Office policies and procedures (i.e., efficient use of the clerical staff).
- Maintenance policies and procedures (i.e., efficient use of the custodial staff).
- Standard operating procedures and duties, related to taking attendance, distributing textbooks, etc.
- Personnel and payroll information, with references to school district documents and offices.
- Student personnel policies and procedures (guidance, discipline, etc.).
- Grading and grade reporting procedures.
- Safety and emergency procedures.
- Other useful information for the success of the teacher.

The handbook for students will contain some of the same items as the teacher handbook, but it will also have some unique items. It is, of course, important that the student handbook be written at an interest and difficulty level appropriate for the students in the school. It is particularly important that the handbook be appealing to students so that they will treat it as a valuable guide and refer to it on a regular basis. A quite useful procedure to enhance this process is to have the classroom teacher or homeroom teacher review some of the important elements of the handbook so that students become familiar with its contents and its value to them as a guide. In fact, in many elementary schools, separate student handbooks are not used; but pertinent student information is contained in the teachers' handbook so that they can disseminate it appropriately to the students.

A student handbook might include the following items:

- A welcome and an introduction to the school.
- An introduction to the school's teachers, administrators, counselors, office personnel, and custodial personnel.
- A map of the school.
- The daily schedule of the school.
- The school calendar.
- Academic expectations.
- Curricular and extracurricular opportunities.
- Grading procedures.
- Emergency procedures.
- Discipline policy.
- Dress and grooming expectations.
- Care and maintenance of school facilities, textbooks, etc.
- Cafeteria services
- Student lockers
- Attendance
- Homework and makeup work
- Other useful information for the success of the student at school.

It is also useful to have a brochure or handbook available for parents. Such a document can present the school's message to parents and encourage them to become eager and productive partners in the education of their children. It is also valuable for parents whose students enroll in the school during the school year or for parents who are considering buying a home in the community. This document should state, in layman's terms, the vision and mission of the school and should invite parents to visit the school and participate in it. It should describe the curricular and extracurricular opportunities available to their students. It should introduce parents to the school's faculty and staff and tell them whom to contact when they have questions or problems. It should briefly acquaint them with important school policies and procedures, related to attendance, grading, contacts with teachers, etc. It should provide a floor plan and a calendar. It should give a special invitation for them to participate in the school's parent organizations and to support other school activities (e.g., athletics, school play, etc.). In short, the parent handbook or brochure should sell parents on the school.

In most public school districts in America, principals don't have to convince parents to send their students to the school, though, with the expansion of private school and home teaching alternatives, more principals are looking for ways to attract families who take the education of their students seriously and will become valuable partners in the school enterprise. The brochure or handbook should try to convince the parents that this school is the best place their children could possibly be!

But the need goes beyond attracting those "interested" parents. Many parents, particularly minorities and those from lower socio-economic backgrounds, do not feel welcome at the school. Much of this may have nothing to do with the particular school and may be the result of their frustrations with schools that their children attended previously or even be the result of their own experiences when they were in school. These parents also are stakeholders, and the parent brochure or handbook that they receive should make them know that the school is a friendly place in which they and their students are welcome and that invites them to join as partners in their children's education.

## ACTION FOLLOW-UP

♦ Examine the master schedule of a school. Consider the alternative decisions that could have been made about time and space. Write a statement about the educational priorities that are reflected in the master schedule. Compare those priorities with those that are expressed in the school's mission statement. Consider how alternative approaches to scheduling might serve the school's mission.

♦ Examine two successive annual campus plans that your school has produced. Consider how well the second one builds on the first one and how well they both reflect campus strategic planning. Make recommendations for how this planning process can be improved.

♦ Review your school's master calendar. Does it adequately meet the needs of all stakeholders? How might it be improved?

♦ Review handbooks or other documents that your school distributes to teachers, students, and parents. Are these documents written appropriately for their intended audiences? Do they appropriately cover the necessary topics? How could they be improved?

# 5

# SHORT-RANGE PLANNING: MAINTAINING DIRECTION UNDER PRESSURE

The principal's job is a kaleidoscope of fragmented episodes and interrupted communications that encompass the most mundane events of the school day, the patient building of futures for students and staff, and the personal crises of youth and adults. Important jobs that are begun must often be put on hold while requirements of lesser significance encumber the time that had been established for them. The important gives way to the immediate. It is not unusual for a principal to be called out of a curriculum development session with teachers to deal with a fight that has broken out in the halls.

More than twenty years ago, one of the authors wrote this about the principal's job:

> A good measure of the principal's difficulty seems to lie in the fact that such a variety of people have direct access to him. Consider these positions in the school organization: principal, teacher, student, superintendent, parent, concerned citizen. Of these positions, the principal is the only one to whom all the others in the group typically have direct access. Small wonder that he's beleaguered. Small wonder that, even in a time of general educator surplus, it is difficult to find capable people to fill the position. (Erlandson, 1972, p. 2)

Nor has the intensity of the job diminished over the decades. On the contrary, while the flat organizational structure remains that gives scores of people direct access to the principal, the number of responsibilities (special education, bilingual education, drug prevention, etc., etc.) has grown tremendously, and the rapidity of change caused by a turbulent social environment has accelerated in an unprecedented fashion. Organizational literature out of the corporate sector sometimes seems irrelevant and frustrating to the principal. As noted in Chapter 2, a recent study revealed that elementary principals in typical American schools, ranging between 500 and 1000 in student population, are likely to have between 50 and 70 adults reporting directly to them (Erlandson & Lyons, 1995). This "span of control" is considered impossible in most other organizations, but it is what the principal can expect to face. Maintaining one's priorities and adhering to a schedule require a mode of operation that goes well beyond what administrators and managers face in other organizations. The principles that were discussed in Chapter 2 ("A Foundation for Organizational Oversight") are critical when applied to the principal's mastery of what many analysts would call an impossible job. Principals must find a way of making the human organization work for them. Valid information must flow freely across all levels of the school organization, and, somehow, principals must remain abreast of it while not allowing themselves to drown in it. This chapter provides the principal with practical procedures for doing this. However, a word of caution must be given. The specific procedures given are those that have worked for other principals in other situations. While they illustrate principles that have broad applicability, such specific procedures tend to be person and situation specific. We would encourage the principal to experiment with these, modify them, and use them to invent his/her own applications. Only when such procedures are custom-made for a particular principal's job will they be able to provide the benefits they promise.

## CALENDARS

Chapter 4 described the master calendar and its importance for organizing time and human and material resources in the service of the school's mission. The principal must also use a variety of other calendars that will be supplemental to it and fill in the details for the immediate future. These supplementary calendars may include monthly calendars, weekly calendars, a personal calendar, and possibly a variety of other "special" calendars.

Two versions of a monthly calendar should be planned, prepared, and distributed. One of these calendars should be directed primarily to the school staff. It should contain:

♦ All special events, including time, place, and participants.

♦ All regular events, including faculty/staff meetings, committee meetings, campus team meetings, PTA meetings, grade level/department meetings, principals' meetings, parent training, etc.

♦ Special notations such as staff birthdays.

A second monthly calendar should be directed toward parents and the community. This calendar should contain:

♦ All special events, including time, place, and participants.

♦ All regular events, including PTA meetings, campus team meetings, student activities, parent training, adult education classes, etc.

♦ Special Emphases, such as American Public Education Week, Bike Safety Week, etc.

There are a variety of ways to prepare and present monthly calendars. There are many computer software programs that have calendars available. There are also preprinted blank calendars and clip art to add to your own calendar design. Each school should choose a monthly calendar format that best reflects the vision and the "personality" of the school. More than anything else the monthly calendar should reflect what the school values. It is asking its audiences, whether staff, parents, or community, to pay attention to what the school believes is important.

The weekly calendar is primarily an internal document, designed to give faculty and staff an overview of what the principal will be involved in during the week and to help them organize their week and organize their own work schedules to mesh with the principal's. It is an invaluable aid for getting everyone started on the same page on a Monday morning. It can be used as part of a weekly bulletin that may include a motivational thought and highlight important reminders for the week. "Congratulations" and "thank you's" can also be communicated through this vehicle.

Specifically, the weekly calendar should facilitate the following:

♦ It should let the faculty and staff know of commitments that may take the principal, assistant principals, or other office personnel off campus during the week. This information helps them in scheduling needed conferences with the principal, arranging for the principal to visit their classrooms, etc.

♦ The weekly calendar is also designed to keep the faculty and staff aware of what the principal is doing when she or he is not on campus. This makes them feel informed and that they are a part of the larger school district picture.

♦ The weekly calendar provides the principal with a week long snapshot and thus enables more efficient scheduling of time on campus. It helps the principal organize time so that he/she can better schedule classroom visitations and attend to the other normal daily demands.

♦ It enables the principal to be more accountable for allocation of time across the week and provides the principal with a record of where his/her time and energy are being directed.

In secondary schools, weekly activity calendars are also often developed and published, primarily for the purpose of keeping students and staff aware of the various student activities that are taking place on the campus or in other settings. Such weekly schedules, like the regular weekly calendar, add to feelings of organizational cohesiveness by making everyone aware of what the school family is doing.

The principal also needs to maintain a personal calendar. Different calendars are available that emphasize different time periods and are conducive to handling different pieces of information. DayRunner books, electronic pocket-sized calendars, and laptop personal computers with calendar options are a few of the alternatives that are available. The principal should select a personal calendar format, depending on whether he/she prefers to plan and monitor primarily on a daily, weekly, or monthly basis. The principal should take care to make entries in the calendar at the time that appointments are made or the calendar is otherwise encumbered. Given the hectic schedules of most principals, leaving times and appointments to memory, even for a relatively short time, is very dangerous.

The principal should work directly with a secretary in maintaining a personal calendar. Two identical calendars should be maintained: one that is kept in the office and one that goes with the principal. In fact, no calendar option is worth the money or time invested in it unless both the secretary and the principal use it! In the kaleidoscopic world of the principal's job, there must be a lot of communication between principal and secretary in order to maximize the use of everyone's time.

## MAKING THE CALENDAR WORK FOR YOU

### "To Do" Lists

"To Do" lists can be extremely valuable organizers for the principal and can be incorporated into the workday in several ways. They can be tied directly to the calendar by assigning time in the day to attend to different tasks. They can be used as a separate list and referred to during the day on an ongoing basis. The principal can develop a personal coding system. For example, he/she might put a check mark next to an item for which appropriate action has been initiated (e.g., asking the secretary to pull together a set of materials that the principal will need to draft a memo to the assistant superintendent). When the memo has been written and sent, the item on the "To Do" list may be lined out. Some principals prefer a more complex system, using task books/notebooks that help distinguish between items that are critical, pending, or can be done when time allows. Obviously, the more comprehensive the system, the more it tells the principal and serves as an aid to organization. On the other hand, it takes additional time to maintain a complex system. Each principal needs to find a system that works best for him or her.

One of the authors, who has been both an elementary principal and a secondary principal, established this routine for organizing her day:

- Plans her day in her DayRunner with scheduled appointments or meetings.
- Makes a list of work that requires immediate attention.
- Identifies work that has an immediate deadline and work that has an extended deadline. Then sets intermediate deadlines for herself to ensure that work is done.
- Determines whether the work is something she needs to do by herself or if it is work that needs to be done jointly with the Campus Site-Based Team, with other school committee personnel, or with other individuals. Then schedules appropriate meetings so that the tasks can be completed.
- Delegates the work that someone else can do.
- Mentally plans the day so that she can set some reasonable goals for completion during the day.
- Is prepared to depart from the schedule in order to deal with crisis interruptions.
- After interruptions, gets back on schedule as much as possible.

A similar routine, organized to meet the needs of the particular principal, would probably be in order for any principal at any level of schooling.

The principal's "to do" list, tied directly to the principal's calendar, should provide enough space to accommodate both items that need immediate attention and work that does not need immediate attention. While much of a principal's routine paperwork (reports, letters, district policy statements, state regulations, etc.) does not require immediate attention, it generally comes on a regular basis and must be handled carefully. The fact that it is not immediate does not mean that it is unimportant. While some principals leave all their paperwork until the building is fairly empty at the end of the day or until the first thing in the morning before the students arrive, we would recommend that the principal plan on some space in the day for addressing this work. There are two reasons for this recommendation. First, if the principal is to continue to make a positive impact on the school organization and the people in it, he or she needs a life outside of the school. Most principals will have more than enough of their time beyond the regular school day encumbered by evening school-related activities, without filling the intervening time with paperwork. Principals need a time for personal renewal, and summer vacations alone cannot provide it for the duration of a school year or the duration of a career. Second, there will be many totally unforeseen events during the school day that are relatively time-consuming and must be handled immediately. If there is no space in the day to accommodate these events, scheduled activities will suffer. If space is provided in the day, it can be used either for routine paperwork or for unforeseen events that demand immediate attention. If these unforeseen events use up the space, then the paperwork can be done after school or before school in the morning. This type of contingency planning can make a much more reasonable day and provide for a much more reasonable lifestyle for the principal. The professional's contribution to the education of society's youth is not measured over the space of a day or even a year but over the length of a career.

Space should also be provided in the day for returning phone calls. These phone calls come from a multitude of sources. Most people who take the trouble to call the principal at work believe that their messages are of fairly great importance. Nothing can destroy the credibility of a principal and the school faster, with parents, professionals, and other stakeholders, than unreturned phone calls. Some principals find it useful to set aside a certain time each day for returning phone calls (perhaps right after lunch). While we would not want to prescribe a specific time for every principal, we do feel it is extremely important that some time be set aside to respond to these important links with the organization's environment. If the principal cannot return a call in a timely manner, or if someone else in the organization can handle it better, the task may be passed on to assistants or even the school secretary. The chief concern is that the person who has initiated the contact feels that the school is truly a responsive organization.

While we believe, as stated earlier, that the principal should not have all of his or her waking hours occupied with school matters, it is important for the principal to realize that many things can be better handled outside of the regular school day. Some of the school's stakeholders will not be available until after the regular work day. Also, critical meetings with individuals and groups are likely to be more productive in the quiet, uninterrupted time that a meeting after regular school hours allows. The principal will want to make judicious use of this available time after school.

## USING YOUR SECRETARY

Your secretary should be trained to stay on schedule with all events and appointments. Each afternoon your secretary can provide you with a 3x5 card listing all appointments for the next day. This little reminder will help you organize your day and allows for last minute adjustments, particularly if an appointment requires that you have specific information in front of you. Your secretary can help provide information for conferences and appointments, if she is aware of them, by providing you with student data, correspondence, or other pertinent information.

Parent conferences are a special concern for the principal and should be organized for their maximum effectiveness. Sometimes parents are reluctant to disclose the reason for their visit, and in order to make them feel at ease, it might be useful for you to have your secretary assemble a standardized "parent folder" for any visit that might include the following:

♦ Student's school records, including student enroll-ment card, grade report, attendance report, and discipline record.

- Medical history, special education records, or anything else that you and your secretary deem as appropriate material for a parent conference.

Having this folder prepared in advance will save you the lost time of having someone get it during the conference. It will also avoid an unnecessary interruption in your conversation with the parent.

While the elementary principal is likely to handle these parent conferences at his/her own desk, with the parent folder available for reference, most parent conferences at the secondary level are more likely to be initially handled by an assistant principal, perhaps in conjunction with a counselor or the registrar. However, the concept of a parent folder is equally applicable in a middle school or high school. The principal can bring some quality control to this important communication link by establishing a general system for anyone who comes into contact with parents. If the school has its student files on a computerized system that allows immediate access to all the pertinent information by personal computer, this general system will be relatively easy to implement.

A variety of other types of appointments can also affect your ability to manage your schedule. These include conferences with sales persons, other school district personnel, community leaders, etc. In order to be prepared for these visits, it will help if you or your secretary have some prior knowledge of the reason for the visit. This information is not always available, but with some preplanning a folder can be prepared containing general information about the campus, a copy of the campus plan, a list of the staff, and other similar information. Such ready information can facilitate discussion and maximize the use of both your time and your visitor's.

It is extremely helpful if you can work out a system that allows your secretary to keep you on task. Some of the following suggestions might be used, with, of course, the necessary modifications to make them appropriate for your situation.

- Have your secretary advise you of meetings off campus 15 minutes before you need to leave so that you can wrap up whatever you're doing (e.g., bring a conference to a close or complete a phone call).

♦ Control the length of a conference that you suspect may run unnecessarily long because of the personalities involved. One way this can be done is to schedule another appointment (e.g, another conference or a classroom observation) at a reasonable time following the conference. Notify the conference participants of this scheduled commitment at the beginning of the conference so that they can allocate their time appropriately. Also, have your secretary remind you of the commitment 15 minutes in advance. In this way the conference can be handled in an orderly and efficient manner, and no one is offended or left with the impression that you consider their agenda unimportant. If the time allotted is genuinely too short for handling substantive matters, another conference can be scheduled.

♦ A car phone can be very useful. While returning to the school after a meeting or traveling between meetings, it can be extremely helpful to call the school so that your secretary can alert you to upcoming appointments, let you know that a particular individual is waiting to talk to you, or tell you that you need to call someone as soon as possible. Taking care of some of these calls while en route will help you use that time efficiently and decreases the number of calls that are waiting for you when you return to your office. Similarly, being aware of other developments at the school enables you to develop at least a general strategy for dealing with them when you return.

♦ Using the daily 3x5 card that your secretary has prepared for you can help you handle your daily commitments efficiently and plan appropriately for after-school meetings as you go about your busy schedule. The information on the card should include daytime events as well as evening commitments, with appropriate names, addresses, and phone numbers. The card should also give one- or two-word reminders of the nature of appointments, birthdays of staff, and "pending folder" items.

Use your secretary not only to keep you on track during the day and the week, but also to organize the office so that it runs smoothly without your constant attention and, when necessary, in your absence. The secretary should know the organization so well that he/she can route telephone calls to the proper person (assistant principal, counselor, etc.) even when the caller cannot identify who the appropriate person is. Such valuable "gatekeeping" functions can add great efficiency to the organization. For example, if the secretary merely takes the message for the principal to return a call and if the principal, upon returning the call finds that someone else in the organization (perhaps even the secretary) could handle the matter as well or better, the principal's valuable time has been unnecessarily encumbered, or truly wasted, if the principal him/herself must serve as gatekeeper and route the call to the appropriate party. Mail and visitors to the office can be efficiently routed to the appropriate persons if the secretary is an effective office manager.

## COMMUNICATING THROUGH TEAMS

Throughout this book we have emphasized the principal's use of teams to plan, communicate, and implement activities in the school. This team principle applies as much to maintaining daily and weekly direction as it does to other areas of the school's operation. However, these short-range planning teams are likely to be more specifically task-oriented and are not likely to be identical with the teams that the principal uses for other purposes, though many of the individual members may be the same. Furthermore, in a secondary school there may be more than one of these teams, with team composition determined by its specific task orientation. On these short-range planning teams the principal will want primarily those persons whose formal positions in the organization bring them into contact with the school's major audiences (assistant principals, department chairs, counselors, etc.). The purpose of these teams is to provide quick two-way communication on what is happening in the school and what should be done now to prepare and/or respond to it.

With calendars in front of them, a short-range planning team (made up of assistant principals and/or other key communicators) should meet on a weekly or biweekly basis to prepare for what is happening in the days immediately ahead. Such meetings allow the team (1) to line up the operation of the school with scheduled events— checking who is on duty, what events are being held in the building, etc.; (2) to discuss any ongoing problems in an attempt to prevent difficulties that team members anticipate; (3) to discuss any unusual personnel problems or "gossip" that team members need to be aware of in order to prevent rumors and otherwise provide faculty and other stakeholders with the necessary information to prevent disruption.

In a similar manner, other team meetings are held on a regular basis for specific functions. Weekly meetings should be held with department or grade-level chairs. At these meetings, concerns are raised about the educational program, and school and district policy are integrated with the delivery of instruction. Counselors and other school professionals also need to be part of school teams that meet on a regular basis in order that their specific functions and activities are integrated with the other functions and activities of the school. Teams, as we have repeated throughout the book, enhance communication by providing multiple channels to the school's various audiences and engender empowerment by enlisting key members of the school organization as integral parts of the process by which school decisions are made and implemented.

## BUILDING SKILL IN SHORT-RANGE PLANNING: IN-BASKET EXERCISES

In this chapter we have emphasized the fragmented and hectic nature of the principal's job. We have also suggested some tools and techniques for helping the principals stay on top of the changing situations that they face. We would like now to give you a chance to practice applying principles of daily planning and to assess your skills in this crucial area. We propose to do this by providing two modified in-basket exercises: one built on an elementary principal's work and one built on a high school principal's position. Unlike the typical in-basket, you will not be asked to actually write letters or take actions. Instead, these modified in-baskets only ask for a description of the action taken or to be taken and a short reason why it was done. This approach emphasizes two features of much of the advice given in this chapter: (1) the principal must assign proper priority and make good decisions about diverse topics in a limited period of time, and (2) the principal must base these decisions on solid organizational principles.

Figures 5.1 (see pages 118–119) and 5.2 (see pages 123–124) provide worksheet forms that should used in completing these exercises. Each worksheet has two columns: an "Action Taken" column and a "Reason for Action" column. In the proper space in the first column, indicate the action you would take. For instance, in the "Action Taken" column you might write comments like the following:

"I would ask the teacher to see me sometime before the end of the day. When we met I would give her a Xeroxed copy of the applicable part of the board's policy."

"I would call the Assistant Superintendent and ask that the deadline for our campus report be extended until after tomorrow's meeting with parent representatives."

In the second column, indicate why you have taken the action indicated in the first column. For instance, in the "Reason for Action" column you might write comments like the following:

"The matter is critical and must be taken care of immediately. The teacher needs to know board policy so that she can make a proper choice in the matter."

"Unless there are compelling reasons to the contrary, the Assistant Superintendent should prefer a good report a day late rather than a partial report on time."

After you have looked over Figure 5.1 or 5.2, you are ready to begin one of the exercises. You will have 30 minutes to complete the exercise. Read over the incidents presented in the exercise and describe your actions and reasons for action in the appropriate spaces on one of the tables. After you have completed the exercise (or at the end of 30 minutes if you are unable to complete the exercise), stop working and begin comparing your answers with those provided on the pages immediately following the two exercises.

It is recommended that you do this exercise as part of a group of principals or persons who are preparing for the principalship. After you have all completed the exercise, it will be useful to compare your responses with each other's and with those that are given in the appropriate section below entitled either "Discussion: Happy Valley Elementary School" or "Discussion: Edgemont High School."

## IN-BASKET 1

*Happy Valley Elementary School*

You, Greta Marcus, principal of Happy Valley Elementary School, return to your office after two days at a statewide principals convention. You arrive at the school half an hour before the students start arriving, at which time you would like to be at the front door and in the front hall to greet the students and help them and the teachers get ready for the day. You have half an hour to look over the items that arrived while you were gone and integrate them into the plan for the day. The 10 items below are in your in-basket. Indicate on Figure 5.1 what action you will take for each of these items and the reason for each of your actions. At the end of 30 minutes, stop working on the exercise and compare your answers with those provided in the "Happy Valley Elementary School Analysis."

- Mr. Joe Rice, school board member, called while you were out. He has been invited by your PTA president to attend the next PTA meeting and address the issue of his upcoming election. He would like for you to call him and provide him with the names of parents and staff who would work a table for him at your school on election day.

- Janice Jones, a special education teacher, has left you a note saying that she is not happy with her appraisal and would like to meet with you. The district's mandated appraisal period ended while you were attending the conference.

- On your desk you find a recent letter from the state education agency providing you with a report on their recent accreditation visit to your campus. They have asked that your campus team provide a written response to their recommendations within seven days. Your spring break begins in three days and all of your staff will be off duty for a week.

- A parent, Mrs. Viera, has come by the office with a complaint that her son is being taken advantage of by older students after school. She alleges that her son is being bullied and is having to "pay off" older students to allow him to go home safely.

- The superintendent's secretary has called to inform you that you are expected to attend a two-day conference on restructuring at the central office beginning tomorrow at 8:00 A.M.

- The second grade teachers have told the secretary that they need to meet with you as soon as possible to discuss the new test specifications for math at the second grade level. They are to attend a staff development session the day after next and would like to see you before they go.

- The plant services manager called and left a message that the work scheduled to be done on your school flooring during spring break will have to be rescheduled. Your custodians have arranged their workweek to accommodate the prescheduled work and want to meet with you to discuss their vacation schedules, which are due in Central Office by 4:00 today.

- The Retired Teachers' Association has written you that they want to honor one of your teachers at their next meeting. They need a letter of recommendation from you by noon tomorrow so that it can be printed in their program.

- The PTA president (new to the job) wants to have a fundraiser immediately after spring break. He has asked that a candy salesman come to the school today at 2:45 P.M. today and would like for you to be present at the meeting.

- The school secretary is retiring after 27 years of service to the school. She has told the Courtesy Committee that she does not want a retirement party. The Courtesy Committee chairperson has left a note on your desk asking you to talk to the secretary because the school wants to schedule a dinner in May and committee members are afraid that they won't be able to get a reservation if they have to wait until after spring break.

## FIGURE 5.1. HAPPY VALLEY ELEMENTARY SCHOOL: RESPONSES TO IN-BASKET

| Action Taken | Reasons for Action |
| --- | --- |
| 1. Joe Rice, School Board Member | 1. |
| 2. Janice Jones, Teacher | 2. |
| 3. State Education Agency Letter | 3. |
| 4. Mrs. Viera | 4. |
| 5. Restructuring Conference | 5. |

| Action Taken | Reasons for Action |
|---|---|
| 6. Second Grade Teachers Meeting | 6. |
| 7. Plant Service Manager | 7. |
| 8. Retired Teachers' Association | 8. |
| 9. PTA President | 9. |
| 10. School Secretary Retirement | 10. |

## IN-BASKET 2

### *Edgemont High School*

You, Steve Harper, principal of Edgemont High School, return to your office after two days at a statewide principals convention. You arrive at the school half an hour before the formal start of the school day at 8 A.M. You will have to leave the building at that time for a conference with the Assistant Superintendent for Curriculum and Instruction related to the trimester scheduling plan that your school will adopt in the Fall semester. You have half an hour to look over the items that arrived while you were gone and integrate them into the plan for the day. The 10 items below are in your in-basket. Indicate on Figure 5.2 what action you will take for each of these items and the reason for each of your actions. At the end of 30 minutes, stop working on the exercise and compare your answers with those provided in the "Edgemont High School Analysis."

- ♦ Mrs. Anderson, the grandmother of a new student has called in to leave the message that her grandson was involved in a fight and was placed in the school district's alternative learning center by the assistant principal. (This is the prescribed consequence in the school's student discipline handbook.) She maintains that her grandson, as a new student, was never given a handbook nor were the discipline guidelines explained to him.

- ♦ An angry parent, Mrs. Butler, has left a message that her daughter's name was left off the ballot for senior class student council elections. Since you were out of the building when she stopped by yesterday, she has requested that you call her sometime today. An accompanying note from Fred Geyer, the student council sponsor, informs you that the girl's name was not listed as the result of an inadvertent mistake by the student who had prepared the ballots. However, the election has been completed, and the positions have been filled. He would like your advice on how to solve this problem.

♦ The Director of Secondary Education for the Edge-mont School District has called to remind you that you are scheduled to attend a two-day planning session next week at the central office and that you will be out of your school for that period. A glance at your schedule shows you that next week promises to be a particularly busy one that involves a number of schoolwide events that will require coordination.

♦ Sally Sassy, a teacher who has been given a teaching reassignment for next year, has scheduled a meeting with you for 10 A.M. this morning. She has indicated that at the meeting she wishes to challenge her reassignment and will be accompanied by the building union representative. You were aware of the appointment before you left for the principals convention, but you haven't had much chance to think about it. You originally made the decision for Ms. Sassy's reassignment because of the number of students who had withdrawn from the program during the current year, and in making the reassignment you carefully followed the district's guidelines for reassignment of teachers. You know, however, that this is a delicate situation and that you must carefully consider how you will approach the meeting with Ms. Sassy.

♦ The school district's custodial director has left a message that the gym floors will be refinished the last week in June. Your basketball coach has scheduled a basketball camp for that week and there has already been a preregistration for it.

♦ A note from your secretary tells you that a concerned parent has informed her that the date for Homecoming in the Fall semester is the same weekend as Yom Kippur. Your community has a sizable number of Jewish families.

♦ The school nurse informs you that there are students not current with their shot records. She has documentation that she has sent two letters to each student but has had no response.

- The registrar leaves a message concerning a new student who had been enrolled by bringing a hand-carried copy of his transcript from an American school in Germany. Upon receipt of the official transcript from the former school, it is discovered that the official transcript and the hand-carried transcript do not match. The official transcript shows that the student failed subjects that the hand-carried document shows as having been passed. The parents vouch that to the best of their knowledge the hand-carried transcript is correct.

- There is a message from the senior counselor that a senior boy expecting to graduate is one-half credit short of graduation requirements and it is now the middle of the Spring semester.

- Your secretary has left a note that the parents of a junior girl are coming to visit you this afternoon regarding sexual harassment at school of their daughter by her former boyfriend.

## FIGURE 5.2. EDGEMONT HIGH SCHOOL: RESPONSE TO IN-BASKET

| Action Taken | Reasons for Action |
|---|---|
| 1. Mrs. Anderson, Grandmother | 1. |
| 2. Mrs. Butler, Angry Parent | 2. |
| 3. Two Day Planning Session | 3. |
| 4. Sally Sassy | 4. |
| 5. Refinishing the Basketball Floor | 5. |

| Action Taken | Reasons for Action |
|---|---|
| 6.  Yom Kippur | 6. |
| 7.  Shot Records | 7. |
| 8.  New Student from Germany | 8. |
| 9.  One-half Credit Short | 9. |
| 10.  Sexual Harrassment | 10. |

## IN-BASKET 1: DISCUSSION

### Happy Valley Elementary School

The following analysis of the Happy Valley Elementary School in-basket items has been provided as a guide for analyzing your own actions and the reasons you took them. Your actions and reasons may be different in particulars from those proposed and still be appropriate, but they must be supported by logic and principle, just as these are. Compare your responses not only with the proposed solutions given below, but also with the responses of other persons in the group who have taken the exercise. Discuss the impact of various actions not only in terms of the particular problem to which they are addressed but to the principal's entire job and work schedule. Each of the numbered sections responds to the corresponding item in the in-basket.

### 1. Joe Rice, School Board Member

There are two issues involved in the situation with the board member, Joe Rice. The first issue involves working with the PTA president in planning monthly meetings and setting appropriate agendas. It is important to work as closely with the PTA as possible and help them make appropriate decisions. One way to do this is to schedule monthly meetings prior to the regularly scheduled meeting to discuss the upcoming agenda. During this meeting you could use a planning agenda worksheet that would help keep the president focused and perhaps prevent situations like this one from happening. Setting the program agenda at the beginning of the year also helps the PTA set parameters for their meetings and precludes them from becoming "soapboxes" for political candidates or special interest groups. Setting the agenda for the year together, as an executive council, enables everyone to be a part of the planning process and share in decision making.

Return the board member's call at a time convenient for you. Let him know that you cannot provide him with any names to work for him on election day, but since he has been invited to come to the PTA meeting, he can invite volunteers to join him at his headquarters if they are interested in helping on election day. By returning his call, you are responding to him as a courtesy, but you are not volunteering any staff member or parent to actively participate in his campaign.

Call the PTA president as soon as possible and invite him to come and discuss the situation. At that time, share with him your concern that the school and the PTA be viewed as being fair to all candidates and that the other candidates must be invited to speak if there are others running for the same position.

If Mr. Rice is running unopposed, then you can probably let the invitation stand. You can encourage your PTA president to use the time as forum for the parents and community to let Mr. Rice know of concerns they might have regarding the school district. At that time the school staff and PTA should be ready to recommend solutions for some of the problems they raise so that the PTA is seen as a positive force in the community.

By scheduling regular planning sessions with the PTA president, the situation encountered in this case could probably be avoided. If the request did come to the president, the agenda for the meeting would already be set and any requests to add to the agenda could be referred to the executive council where all the pros and cons could be discussed. As the school principal, you could help facilitate the discussion so that the PTA could avoid unnecessary conflict or criticism.

In a nutshell: Preplanning is a must!

a. Plan ahead. Have a process in place that provides for constant communication and planning with the PTA president.

b. Return phone calls promptly and be honest about what you can or can't do.

c. Involve others in the planning and decision-making process; everyone needs a vested interest in the success of the entire school program.

d. Actively protect and support the leaders in your school community so they grow in stature and are viewed as being effective by others.

## 2. Janice Jones, Teacher

Place a note in Janice's box and ask her to come by the office during her next conference period (provide date and time) so that you can explore the options that you both have in regard to her appraisal. For the conference have the following ready:

a. A copy of the appraisal calendar and the district and state guidelines for appeals.

b. A copy of the appraisal.

c. A list of some of the options that you think are viable.

In a nutshell: Preplanning is a must!

a. Publish your appraisal calendar so that everyone is aware of the deadlines involved.

b. Schedule your own time so that you can conference with all employees within the required time limits.

c. Research the options that are available to both of you that are within state and district policy.

## 3. State Education Agency Letter

Establish a time and convene the campus leadership team (or some similar body if you have one) and provide them with a copy of the letter from the agency. Ask them to divide into their standing committees and divide up the report so that every committee can respond to a particular area. Each committee should be given a half-day to work on their responses. Then use a process that will facilitate reaching consensus on key issues. A previously identified writing team can then take the work of the committees and bring back a draft of the responses right after spring break. Notify the agency and let them know that your report will be forthcoming but that it will not be within the 7-day time frame. Tell them that they will have it within 10 working days.

In a nutshell: Preplanning is a must!

a. Actively involve everyone in the planning process by requiring that the entire campus be a part of a standing committee that is directly tied to the campus plan.

b. Model and facilitate a consensus model for decision making so that everyone is involved and committed to the success of the plan.

c. Build in an evaluation component and time for dialogue so that self-assessment comes naturally to all members of the staff.

d. Utilize the talents of all members of the faculty and place them in positions on committees that will strengthen them individually and collectively.

e. Don't be afraid to say to state agencies or whomever: "This timeline will not work for us because…, but we will be able to provide…by…(a proposed date)." What's the worst that can happen if you do this? In most cases, state agencies and other bureaucracies are well aware of the delays caused by their own ineptitude and will be quite pleased to get a quality response to their request by a date not too long after the "deadline."

f. Utilize time wisely but don't sacrifice school personnel, personal energy, time, or commitment to simply make an unrealistic deadline unless it is truly a matter of life and death. (Most of the time it isn't.) Failure to plan appropriately and implement with all deliberate speed can throw everyone into a panic and produce a substandard product.

g. Set reasonable goals, priorities, and time lines. Build in timely evaluation and assessment components. Involve everyone in the work.

## 4. Mrs. Viera

Ask an administrative assistant, or someone assigned to this duty, to talk with Mrs. Viera, get the details of her complaint, and follow-up with the students involved. Ask to be notified of the outcome of the conference, but don't get involved yourself unless there are extenuating circumstances. If you do not have an administrative assistant or someone assigned to this duty, or if this person is not available, call Mrs. Viera, get the details from her, contact the students involved, and take the appropriate action.

In a nutshell: Preplanning is a must!

a. Train office staff to fill out a "complaint form" whenever a parent calls with a concern. On the form include the following:

   (1) Nature of concern/reason for call.

   (2) Names of all parties involved.

   (3) Place and time of the incident (if at all possible).

   (4) Any other comments that the parent feels are important.

   (5) Action taken by the office.

b. When you call the parent, you should already have talked to the parties involved (assuming they have been identified) and have taken appropriate action according to your school's discipline plan. If you don't have all the information needed, use your available time to investigate so that when you talk to the parent you can deal with as many facts as possible and not pure emotion. Depending on the severity of the complaint, a follow-up conference may be scheduled.

c. When the complaint has been fully investigated, parents have been called, and consequences have been determined, the form is filed in a discipline folder for future documentation. (All of this can be handled on a computer as well, if the school is networked, and can be an integral part of the schoolwide discipline plan.)

## 5. Restructuring Conference

Attend the restructuring conference and ask your administrative assistant, or whoever is in charge while you are gone, to follow up on the list of concerns that were identified at the last staff meeting. Tell that individual that you will check in with him or her during the day and, if necessary, will return to the school at the end of the day to address any concerns that cannot be handled by campus personnel.

In a nutshell: Preplanning is a must!

a. Plan each week for a staff meeting with the administrative team. That may be only you and your secretary, or it may involve any number of people.

    b.  At that meeting, look at schedules, plan for upcoming events or assignments, talk through problem areas, and be supportive of all the efforts of each staff member.

    c.  When you are working from a team concept, it is easier to be "pulled away" on a special assignment if you have been keeping one another informed on a regular basis. It also helps those who are left "in charge" to know that you will be checking in on a regular basis and that they can check with you on issues if they have questions. Depending on the level of trust and ability, you can delegate a great deal, particularly when everyone feels that he/she is an important part of the team and has been empowered to act.

## 6. Second Grade Teachers Meeting

Since your schedule is tight, write a brief note to the second grade teachers and give them some options: (a) they can come in for an early morning meeting before you have to go to the superintendent's office; (b) they can write down their concerns and you can fax them a response; (c) they can meet with the administrative assistant; or (d) they can write down their concerns for you to take to your meeting and schedule a conference with you after spring break.

In a nutshell: Preplanning is a must!

    a.  Communication must be constant and consistent. When you involve everyone, you must be willing to hear concerns as well as ideas.

    b.  Establish a pattern of behavior so that staff can depend on your feedback as well.

## 7. Plant Service Manager

Meet with the custodians at a time that is convenient for everyone. Make whatever adjustments necessary to complete the work, but still try to meet their personal needs as well.

In a nutshell: Since preplanning doesn't always work, you will have to monitor and adjust to make the most of an emerging situation.

   a. If you have modeled respect and courtesy for employees and they are committed to the campus, they are able to deal more efficiently with change.

   b. All employees need to know and believe that they are valued and that you, the principal, will plead their case if someone else tries to call the shots from outside the building.

   c. Work within the system as much as possible, but do what you think is best for the campus and the individual.

## 8. Retired Teachers' Association

Write the letter at home and fax it to them from the superintendent's office.

In a nutshell: Preplanning is a must!

   a. Maintain a file of letters of recommendation in the computer so that you can easily write or adapt one when it is required.

   b. Never pass up an opportunity to praise someone else's good work. It is a glowing reflection of the campus as well as the individual.

## 9. PTA President

When you call the president to schedule a meeting to discuss your concern regarding the board member, Mr. Rice, let him know that you can't meet at 2:45 but that you will have someone present to represent the campus.

In a nutshell: Preplanning is a must!

   a. Regular meetings with the president should help you work through the unexpected challenges of politics. The president should be encouraged to bring his ideas for the fundraiser to the executive council meeting and should be a part of the agenda. Ideally, there has been advanced planning and the fundraiser is on the Master Calendar.

   b. When the preplanning isn't enough, try to facilitate the process so that the president is successful and the decisions made are for the good of the campus and the community.

10. **School Secretary Retirement.**

Make time to talk with the secretary a priority of the day and try to get a sense of why she does not want a retirement party. Try to help her understand why the staff wants to honor her and enlist her help in suggesting some options that she could live with that will also be acceptable to the staff. Pass those options on to the Courtesy Committee chair so that the committee can work on reservations if they are needed.

In a nutshell: Preplanning is a must!

a. Campus guidelines or bylaws for the Courtesy Committee should be developed and agreed upon by the staff. The committee should then plan and operate within those guidelines.

b. Using the Master Calendar, a date and place should be set at the beginning of the year for the retirement gathering regardless of who is retiring. In this way the date and place is set before anyone knows who is retiring and it doesn't become a personal issue.

## IN-BASKET 2: DISCUSSION

### Edgemont High School

The following analysis of the Edgemont High School in-basket items has been provided as a guide for analyzing your own actions and the reasons you took them. Your actions and reasons may be different in particulars from those proposed and still be appropriate, but they must be supported by logic and principle, just as these are. Compare your responses not only with the proposed solutions given below, but also with the responses of other persons in the group who have taken the exercise. Discuss the impact of various actions not only in terms of the particular problem to which they are addressed, but also on the principal's entire job and work schedule. Each of the numbered sections responds to the corresponding item in the in-basket.

### 1. Mrs. Anderson, Grandmother

There are several issues here. First, your assistant principal has taken an action according to the rules and needs your support. Although the student may not have known about Edgemont's particular policy on fighting, he certainly knew that there would be some consequences. All high schools will have some consequences for such behavior. Second, there must be a real concern for the student; it is to no one's advantage for him to start off in the school on a wrong course. Have your assistant principal arrange a meeting with you, him, the grandmother, and the student. While the school's position must be clearly stated at the meeting, it should also be clear to the grandmother and to the student that the school wants him to succeed. Finally, a breakdown in communication should be avoided if at all possible. It would be useful to have the registrar and the counselor meet with a representative group of teachers to devise a way to ensure that all students coming into the school after school has started receive the same information.

## 2. Mrs. Butler, Angry Parent

There is an immediate issue here and also a longer range issue. First you need to set up a meeting with Fred Geyer, Mrs. Butler, and the girl to explore what can be done to solve the problem. The school has made a mistake and this should not be obscured. Having admitted its mistake, the school should enlist Mrs. Butler and her daughter to help solve the problem. One possibility to avoid the difficulty of holding the election a second time would be to offer her an appointed position on the council, particularly if some functional role (such as parliamentarian) were available. The key thing here is not to diminish the school's error but to use this as a learning experience for the girl and for others about how human errors can be overcome by human collaboration. Fred Geyer also needs to meet with the class sponsors, and the student council officers to review nominating procedures and build checks and balances into the system. Their decisions should be reported to you.

## 3. Two-Day Planning Session

Prior to the beginning of the school year you should have made plans to ensure that lines of communication will operate smoothly and that crises will be handled in your absence. Training assistant principals for various leadership roles is part of your job and is necessary for maintaining an efficient operation on your campus and for each assistant principal's career development. It should be clear which assistant principal will be in charge when you're gone and which responsibilities each of the others will take. If you have given them proper preparation, only a short meeting with them will be necessary to review particular concerns with the activities that will occur during this next absence.

### 4. Sally Sassy

Legally and morally you're probably in the right in what you've done so far in this situation, but it still needs to be handled delicately. For whatever reasons, it is clear that Ms. Sassy has not been functioning effectively as a teacher. An organization, like a society, is judged by how it treats its weakest members. You have an obligation, in all your actions, but particularly in situations like this one, to make a statement by your actions for the moral position of the school. You may not be able to avoid a confrontation in this case, but the tone you set in this meeting should make it clear that you do not seek one. You need to make it clear to Ms. Sassy and the union representative that your decision was not meant as a personal criticism. Don't back away from the position that students come first at Edgemont High School. You have made your decision to save a program that you believe is valuable for the academic achievement and personal success of many students. At the same time make it clear to Ms. Sassy that you are also concerned about her success and that you will do your best to provide help in her new assignment.

### 5. Refinishing the Basketball Floor

Somebody in your school probably made a mistake in this one by not clearing the schedule with the custodial director when the dates were first established for the basketball camp. Nevertheless, the basketball program is important for young students in the community and to cancel it would inconvenience families and disappoint many children. The dates need to be changed, and the custodial director must change his schedule. If the confusion in scheduling was indeed the fault of the school, readily admit your mistake, but don't give ground in your insistence that the floor refinishing be rescheduled.

Direct your athletic director and/or head coaches to make sure in the future that they clear schedules not only with you, but also with custodial and maintenance services whenever a proposed event will encumber the school's facilities.

## 6. Yom Kippur

Once again, you need to do two things in this situation: one thing to handle the immediate problem and another to avoid such problems in the future. First, you should meet with the head football coach, the athletic director, and the student council sponsor to identify another available date for Homecoming. For the future you need to advise the school's athletic personnel and the student council to consult religious calendars and other relevant calendars before setting dates for events such as Homecoming. You should consider making important religious dates part of the school's master calendar for the year. It is imperative to be sensitive to the diversity of the community that the school serves. Sometimes it is also necessary to direct others to be sensitive.

## 7. Shot Records

District policy (and in most cases state law) probably requires that parents be notified that their students will not be able to return to school until the shots are current. However, this is another sensitive issue and must be handled with care. First, ask the nurse to provide the appropriate assistant principal(s) with the students' names and documentation. This is potentially a growth opportunity for assistant principals to develop their human skills and their skills of persuasion and become, at once, advocates for both the school and the students. Assistant principals should work on having a personal influence on students and their families. If there are extenuating circumstances that require special help for students to obtain their shots, an assistant principal can help.

## 8. New Student from Germany

The principal or the registrar should probably call the school in Germany directly. If the school confirms that the official transcript is correct (probably by checking teachers' grade books), the student should then be enrolled in the courses that are needed to overcome the deficiencies. Any further appeal to the former school must come from the parents and the student. Unless the school in Germany provides information to the contrary, the official transcript must be followed to be able to recommend the student for graduation.

## 9. One-half Credit Short

The first thing to do (immediately and before contacting the student or family) is to check and double check the transcript to see if any errors have been made. If the student deviates from the expected pattern of course completion (for instance, if he goes to summer school), the record-keeping system is often challenged and errors are easily made. The principal should work with others in the school and in the central office to develop a grade recording system that minimizes such errors. Few things can be more traumatic to a student and his/her family than to find out that their plans will be completely changed by a course credit deficit. If a careful audit shows that the student is indeed short half a credit, the student and his/her parents should be brought in for a conference in which the principal, him or herself, carefully explains the situation and offers help to the student and family in completing the credit (perhaps during the coming summer) and rearranging their plans.

## 10. Sexual Harassment

If possible, before this afternoon's conference, find out from your assistant principals, counselors, or others in the school what has happened in this case. Once the conference with the parents has started, your primary job will be to listen and learn. After you have heard the parents' story, you need to find out the details of what has happened. This is a serious matter and deserves your full attention. First, you should have an assistant principal investigate the alleged incidents, including taking statements from both parties and contacting the young man's parents. Some behaviors on a school campus are not negotiable, and harassment must be addressed and stopped. You should also consult with the appropriate officials in the district office and work with them to develop a sexual harassment policy (if none exists or the policy needs to be refined), as well as planning staff development and awareness teaching for the student body. It is imperative to have policies that encourage and teach decency. Students and teachers should be part of the planning process for any policies that will affect them.

## ACTION FOLLOW-UP

♦ Develop a personal calendar and "To Do" list system that works for you. If you are currently a principal or in another administrative capacity, make a secretary a part of this system. Work on it over time to get it operating efficiently and effectively.

♦ Develop a system of weekly and monthly calendars designed to serve your school, or identify and implement ways in which your current calendar system may be improved.

♦ With a group of colleagues (e.g., other principals), develop an ongoing dialogue about improving your organizational skills through the use of in-baskets that you prepare yourselves. For example, members of the group could take turns preparing modified in-baskets like the ones presented in this chapter, together with proposed sets of responses to each of the items. These proposed responses, together with the responses suggested by the various group members, could then provide the basis for fertile dialogue on improving essential organizational skills.

# 6

# PLANNING FOR CHANGE

To a degree, all planning is planning for change. That is, the purpose of all planning is to prevent things from becoming what they would be if no interventions were made and to cause things to happen that would not happen if no interventions were made. Planning and change are inextricably intertwined and, as such, are a central part of the principal's job. The principal who wants to increase educational excellence in his/her school will be involved in change. This is true even if the principal merely wishes to maintain the school's current state of excellence, because the people in the organization and the context in which it operates are changing.

## THE COMPLEXITY OF CHANGE

Change is a complex process. Significant change is never brought about by simply initiating an innovation and letting it develop. Educators in the past have failed in their efforts to incorporate change into the schools, primarily because they have underestimated the complexity of the change process. As a result, the landscape of education over the last decades has been littered with the debris of innovations that have failed or been simply abandoned. Many educators have perceived change as a simple linear process, as illustrated in Figure 6.1, whereby an innovation is introduced into the operation of the school and the level of productivity (however measured—improved test scores, better attendance, etc.) goes up!

This perception is partially a result of the fact that professional educators are optimistic idealists; that is, they believe that if something is good for the school and the students in it, everybody will want it and will support it. They often fail to understand that "educational good" is often in the eye of the beholder and different stakeholders will have vastly different perceptions of what is best for the education of the students in the school. They often fail to understand that what is "good" in one sense (e.g., interdisciplinary teaming) may be negative at least in some sense (e.g., learning new interpersonal skills and ways of teaching) for some of the school's key stakeholders (in this case, experienced teachers who had built their careers on a different model). This is part of the larger problem presented in Figure 6.1. The true complexity of significant organizational change is not really understood, and change is seen as a simple, straightforward process.

## FIGURE 6.1. CHANGE AS A SIMPLE LINEAR PROCESS

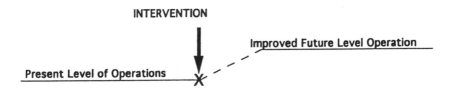

Education is a people endeavor, and significant change in education means that the attitude and behaviors of people will have to change. As every principal knows, the school is made up of diverse people with diverse attitudes and behavior patterns. In addition, there are many people (with different attitudes and priorities) outside the school itself whose support is likely to be crucial for the success of an innovation (superintendent, central office staff, parents, community). There are also material resources that may be essential for the success of an innovation, and, to the degree that they are available, they will also be effectively controlled by people whom the principal must consider in his/her change strategy.

Kurt Lewin (Cunningham, 1982; Lippitt, 1973) envisioned the change process in terms of a force field analysis. (See Fig. 6.2.)

The present state of affairs in any organization are currently held in balance by a set of forces (human and material) that are pressing for change ("driving forces") and a set of forces that are resisting change ("restraining forces"). If we wish to bring about change, we increase the human and material resources (understanding, money, etc.) that support change and reduce or remove those forces (bigotry, misinformation, lack of space) that resist change. This change of balance in opposing forces "unfreezes" the status quo, and enables movement in the desired direction of change. Once the change has been incorporated, steps are taken to "refreeze" the new, desirable situation by stabilizing the new balance of forces.

Yet, even this may be an oversimplification if we stop here in our analysis of the change process. The change process is more than just the straightforward, linear process of adding to positive (driving) forces and reducing negative (restraining) forces (though this is certainly part of it). The school is a system, and all its parts dynamically interact with each other. Forces and persons are interrelated in extremely complex patterns. It is hard to separate cause and effect in a social context. As forces (particularly human forces) move to change elements in the organizational context, they themselves are changed, and their change often produces unanticipated reciprocal changes. This complex interaction must be considered.

Erlandson (1980) has presented a Change Potential Analysis Chart (Fig. 6.3) that may be used to begin analyzing some of this complex interaction. What this chart does is to consider various persons in terms of their functional relation to the change process that is envisioned for a proposed innovation. It identifies these persons and functions, describes their attitudes to the proposed change, considers ways in which the organizational system itself may be used to elicit their support for the change, and identifies ways in which their support will affect other individuals and groups. Figures 6.4, 6.5, and 6.6 provide examples of charts that have been completed for particular innovations in schools.

*(Text continues on page 146.)*

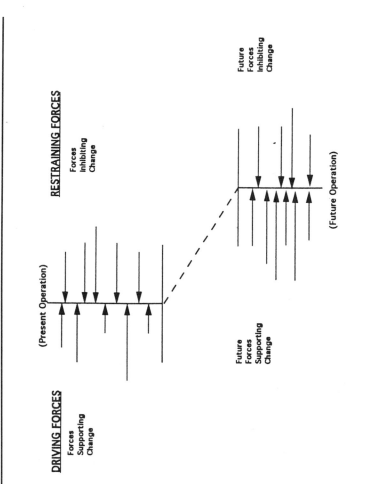

FIGURE 6.2. FORCE FIELD ANALYSIS

## FIGURE 6.3. CHANGE POTENTIAL ANALYSIS CHART

Proposed Change: _____

| | Name Individual(s) or Group(s) | Attitudes Toward Proposed Change | Rewards Sought Through System | How Can These Rewards Be Structured Into Proposed Change? | How Will Support Affect Other Individuals and Groups? |
|---|---|---|---|---|---|
| Formal Decision Maker | | | | | |
| Implementer (s) Of Change | | | | | |
| Other Important Group(s) or Individual(s) (Describe Role In Change Process.) | | | | | |
| Other Important Group(s) or Individual(s) (Describe Role In Change Process.) | | | | | |
| Other Important Group(s) or Individual(s) (Describe Role In Change Process.) | | | | | |

# FIGURE 6.4. CHANGE POTENTIAL ANALYSIS CHART: INSTITUTION OF MULTIDISCIPLINARY INSTRUCTIONAL TEAMS IN HIGH SCHOOL

Proposed Change:  Institution of Multi-Disciplinary Instructional Teams in High School

| | Name Individual(s) or Group(s) | Attitudes Toward Proposed Change | Rewards Sought Through System | How Can These Rewards Be Structured Into Proposed Change? | How Will Support Affect Other Individuals and Groups? |
|---|---|---|---|---|---|
| Formal Decision Maker | High School Principal | Supportive | Professional and personal achievement;Development of a high quality integrated program | Success of innovation; Careful integration of teams into total school program | Positive effect on most teachers; Positive effect on central office administrators, public, and other principals |
| Implementer (s) Of Change | High School Teachers | Mixed; Generally supportive, particularly those teachers to be included on teams | Student achievement; Peer recognition; Professional achievement | Adequate material and moral support to enable success | Generally positive; May cause some alienation of teachers not included |
| Other Important Group(s) or Individual(s) (Describe Role in Change Process.) | Students (Direct Involvement in Implementation) | Essentially uninformed at present; Some concern expressed that subject matter required for college will not be taught | Preparation for college and other post secondary experiences; Peer approval | Develop a quality program that is attractive to student leaders | Positive effect on all other groups |
| | Superintendent (Approval) | Only peripherally concerned at present; Has been mildly supportive | Professional achievement and recognition; Continued tenure | Success fo innovation; Publicity of success | Positive |
| | Assistant Superintendent for Instruction (Approval) | Highly supportive at present (Concept originated here) | Student achievement Professional recognition for high quality program | Structure a positive data collecting, monitoring evaluation, and feedback role | Positive |

# FIGURE 6.5. CHANGE POTENTIAL ANALYSIS CHART: INSTITUTION OF MATH LABS FOR THE EDUCATIONALLY DISADVANTAGED IN THE JUNIOR HIGH SCHOOL

Proposed Change: Institution of Math Labs for the Educationally Disadvantaged in the Junior High School

| | Name Individual(s) or Group(s) | Attitudes Toward Proposed Change | Rewards Sought Through System | How Can These Rewards Be Structured Into Proposed Change? | How Will Support Affect Other Individuals and Groups? |
|---|---|---|---|---|---|
| **Formal Decision Maker** | Junior High School Principal | Positive (Feels that lab approach will enhance the total program in math) | 1. Approval from teachers 2. Professional achievement 3. Recognition from superintendent | Development of a quality program; Publicity of program | Positive |
| **Implementer(s) Of Change** | Teachers in Labs | Positive (Students should benefit from individualized approach) | 1. Peer recognition 2. Superordinate approval 3. Professional achievement | 1. High lab demand 2. Publicity 3. Additional pay for additional time 4. Smaller classes | Positive support from other teachers (Will diminish their problems) |
| **Other Important Group(s) or Individual(s) (Describe Role in Change Process.)** | Regular Classroom Teachers (Support) | Positive (Allow individualization for deficient students) | 1. Professional achievement | Students sent to lab for individual help | Will engender positive support from students and administrators |
| | Students in Labs (Participation) | Negative (Feel stigmatized by class assignment in the labs) | 1. Peer approval 2. Teacher approval 3. Feeling of success 4. Basic skills 5. Good grades | Specific plans to provide students with positive learning experiences and improve students' self-concepts | Positive support would increase teacher support |
| | Other Students (Support) | Neutral | 1. Peer approval 2. Good grades 3. Teacher approval 4. Feeling of accomplishment | 1. Involving all students at some point in the labs 2. Emphasize attractive features of lab | Place pressure on disadvantaged students (?) |

## FIGURE 6.6. CHANGE POTENTIAL ANALYSIS CHART: RESTRUCTURING THE ELEMENTARY SCHOOL IN RESPONSE TO DECLINING RESOURCES

Proposed Change: Restructuring the Elementary School in Response to Declining Resources

| | Name Individual(s) or Group(s) | Attitudes Toward Proposed Change | Rewards Sought Through System | How Can These Rewards Be Structured Into Proposed Change? | How Will Support Affect Other Individuals and Groups? |
|---|---|---|---|---|---|
| Formal Decision Maker | Elementary School Principal | Wants to make restructuring work | Professional and personal achievement; Continuation of excellent educational program | Success of restructuring; Continuation of excellence; Minimization of human suffering | Necessary to enlist support of others; Necessary to retain confidence of superintendent, school board, and parents |
| Implementer (s) Of Change | Teachers and staff retained at school | Want to make restructuring work; Concerns about increased work load; Concern about non-retained colleagues | Professional and personal achievement;Continuatio n of excellent educational program; Professional autonomy | Build collaboration among retained faculty; Build autonomy, personal efficacy, and ownership into restructuring plan | Absolutely essential to make restructured program work and to retain confidence of parents, students, superintendent and school board |
| Other Important Group(s) or Individual(s) (Describe Role in Change Process.) | Teachers and staff not retained at school | Negative about non-retention; Generallysupportive of school program | Sense of professional and personal achievement; Maintenance of sense of personal worth and dignity | Provide recognition of work achieved; Accept negative feelings; Emphasize retention of strong friendship bonds. | Very positive effect on teachers and staff who will be retained; Generally positive on all groups |
| | Students | Want a quality educational program in a clean safe environment | Educational achievement; Maintenance of sense of growth and a feeling of self-worth | Continue educational excellence; Maintain strong personal contacts between teacher and students | Active support of students will do more than anything else to enlist support of other groups |
| | Parents | Want a quality educational program for children in a clean, safe, environment | Educational achievement of students; Happy successful children | Continue educational excellence; Foster relationships between school and parents; | Positive interactive effects on all groups, especially students |

Fullan (1993, pp. 21–41) has more recently examined the complexity of the change process in depth. From his analysis of this complexity he draws eight interrelated lessons regarding the change process. These are summarized here briefly:

Lesson One: *You Can't Mandate What Matters*

Significant changes are complex, and complex change requires (1) new skills, (2) new behaviors, and (3) new beliefs or understanding. Mandates can work when they are applied to things that (1) don't require thinking to accomplish and that (2) can be monitored through close surveillance. An example of a mandate that works relatively well would be a state's compulsory attendance law and the dollars to local school districts that are used to promote compliance. However, significant changes are much more complex and require the thinking and support of the people in the process. This can't be mandated. When mandates are tightened, educational goals are narrowed and the heart is taken out of a complex process.

Lesson Two: *Change Is a Journey Not a Blueprint*

Because of the complex, nonlinear interrelationships that comprise any organization, the change process is never completely predictable. It is the shared vision of where they are going that enables the organization's members to take necessary detours that ultimately ensure the successful completion of the journey.

Lesson Three: *Problems Are Our Friends*

Since the change process is complex, problems are inherent in it. Each problem, rather than being an unwelcome barrier, is a productive challenge that provides organizational members with better insight into the organization and into an understanding of themselves.

Lesson Four: *Vision and Strategic Planning Come Later*

In this book we have repeatedly emphasized the importance of vision and strategic planning. But vision and strategic planning, without a base of shared experience, are likely to be sterile and actually obstructive. This is the reason that we have proposed a "humble decision making" process for strategic planning that gets smarter as it progresses, and a vision building process that is based on the maximization of valid information and the placement of ownership and control of the process in the hands of all members. Vision and strategic planning are built on a foundation of shared experience and information.

Lesson Five: *Individualism and Collectivism Must Have Equal Power*

Exclusive individualism leads to isolation of organization members and the destruction of a common effort. Collectivism leads to groupthink and collective irrelevance. A balance must be struck. A shared vision must be constructed, but the constructions of every individual must reflect that person's personal vision and serve the total organization not only by providing resources for the common effort, but also alternatives that can help it adjust its direction.

Lesson Six: *Neither Centralization Nor Decentralization Works*

Much has been written in recent years about the relative merits of centralization or decentralization. Neither stands alone. Both top-down and bottom-up strategies are necessary. This is related to the first lesson ("You Can't Mandate What Matters"). Any innovation faces two opposite threats: subversion and sterility. If, after mandating the specifics of a desired change, the official(s) at the top (whether the state legislature or a building principal) do not monitor the mandate closely, all sorts of things happen that are unrelated to the true purposes of the innovation. The innovation is subverted. If, on the other hand, the officials at the top monitor the innovation too closely, those at the bottom of the hierarchy are so encumbered with regulations that nothing happens at all. This is sterility. The alternative to these two dangers is to create an environment that leads people at the top and the bottom to a shared vision and enables them, through maximizing the flow of valid information, to jointly develop and implement that vision.

Lesson Seven: *Connection with the Wider Environment Is Critical*

As we will note in a later section of this chapter, the school does not exist in a vacuum. Change is dependent not only on what happens in the school but on what happens outside it as well. The central office of the school district, the community, the state department of education, the legislature—all these bodies are important and affect change in the school. Those who would promote change in the school must take into account the interaction that the school has with these forces and others in its environment.

Lesson Eight: *Every Person Is a Change Agent*

People are important, and every person's presence in the organization is a potential source for change. Argyris and Schön's (1974, 1978) Model II, described in Chapter 2, makes clear why we need the ideas, attention, and dedication of every person in the organization if the potential of an innovation is to be maximized.

Schools are complex, and the educational process itself is complex. It is more than any one person can master or control. Planned change must take this complexity into account and maximize the potential of the school's human resources if the journey of educational change is ever to reach its destination.

## READINESS FOR CHANGE

Since change in a school, as in any other organization, depends upon people, whether a change is incorporated and how faithfully and rapidly it is incorporated will depend on their readiness for change. In the post-Sputnik years, when change in schools was receiving renewed attention, Eichholz and Rogers (1964) recommended that consideration be given to models for disseminating change that had been developed and successfully applied in agriculture. This change dissemination model of rural sociology identifies five stages in the process by which an innovation is adopted:

- *Awareness:* The individual learns of the existence of the innovation.
- *Interest:* The individual seeks more information and considers the merits of the innovation.
- *Evaluation:* The individual makes a mental application of the innovation and weighs its merits for his particular situation.
- *Trial:* The individual applies the innovation on a small scale.

♦ *Adoption:* The individual accepts the innovation for continued use on the basis of the previous trial. (Eichholz & Rogers, p. 303)

We might consider this model first in terms of an application in agriculture. Assume that a new hybrid seed corn has become available that promises to significantly increase yield per acre. Mr. Smith, a farmer, is unaware of this new hybrid seed until his county agent tells him and other farmers in the area about it. This brings Smith into the "awareness" stage. Since increased yield per acre is likely to increase his profits, he enters the "interest" stage of the model and seeks more information about it. He then must make an "evaluation" of whether the anticipated benefits outweigh the risks. He is not unhappy with his yield per acre in previous years, and he must decide if he wishes to risk that security against an unproven alternative. He concludes that, in spite of certain doubts, it is worth a "trial" and decides to use the new hybrid seed in one 40-acre plot. He reaps an outstanding harvest in that field and decides to "adopt" the new seed on a regular basis.

Consider an analogous situation in a school. In Chapter 3 we described the hypothetical case of Wilson High School. "Awareness" of the purposes of education and the probable futures of their students produced an "interest" in the Wilson faculty and other stakeholders in better serving the students' lifelong needs. This led to a consideration of alternative ways of meeting those needs and the selection of a preferred alternative ("evaluation") for doing so. A plan of action was put into effect that implemented the proposed alternative in small stages ("trial"), with the expectation that if it were successful as it expanded each year, it would be "adopted" as a permanent feature of the school's educational program.

American agriculture provides what is probably the greatest success story for planned change in our society (and perhaps in any society). The fantastic increases in agricultural productivity that have enabled less than 5% of our population to provide far more food and other agricultural products than the remainder of the population can readily use is a testimony to the effectiveness with which innovations have been disseminated. While it is certainly unfair to compare education with agriculture because of the very different contexts in which they operate, it may be valuable to consider what lessons we in education might learn. It is instructive to note that the mixed-scanning model proposed by Etzioni (1986) follows so closely many of the principles of this very successful model.

One of the problems in considering the process of change in education is that it is sometimes difficult to know what educators mean when they say that an innovation has been adopted. Gallagher (1967) found that biology teachers who had "adopted" the same new curriculum had in fact adapted it in very different ways. In spite of the intentions of the curriculum innovators, quite different things were happening in their separate classrooms. A school district "adopts" a textbook for its third grade students. Some teachers find that it fits their style of teaching and use it enthusiastically. Others dislike it and avoid it or work around it with other materials whenever possible. To what extent has the textbook really been adopted? Computer hardware and software are available in every classroom in the junior high school. All teachers use them but some much more frequently and creatively than others. How would we describe the degree of integration of computers in this school?

## THE CONCERNS-BASED ADOPTION MODEL

Hall and Hord (1987) have proposed a model, the Concerns-Based Adoption Model (CBAM), that examines the change process in terms of the complexities that underlie these questions. They have identified three dimensions for diagnosing the possibilities for change in a particular context, such as a school: (1) Stages of Concern, (2) Levels of Use, and (3) Innovation Configuration. Stages of Concern identify how teachers or others perceive and feel about an innovation. Levels of Use speaks to what a teacher, or another person, is doing or not doing in relation to an innovation. Innovation Configurations describe the operational forms that an innovation takes. The three dimensions are independent and the person or group who would wish to facilitate change must conduct diagnoses on an ongoing basis to see how the three dimensions develop, interact, and shift over time.

Seven Stages of Concern have been identified, with the lowest stage of concern being mere awareness, with little concern. As persons move through the change process, their concerns tend to become more focused. As concerns develop, they tend first to be centered on seeking additional information and then on how the innovation will affect the persons themselves. Further development leads to concern with the efficient and effective management of the tasks associated with the innovation. Finally, mature concerns reflect attention to consequences of the innovation, collaborative relationships in its implementations, and extensions of the innovation.

The Levels of Use follow a parallel course. From complete "nonuse" an individual progresses through "orientation" and "preparation," two stages in which a person is still technically a nonuser, but moving toward use. Early use tends to be "mechanical use," depending heavily on specific directions and guidelines associated with the innovation. Further involvement leads to "routine" use of the innovation and then possibly to "refinement," where adaptations are made to increase the impact of the innovation on clients. At the "integration" level the user is combining his/her own efforts with related activities of colleagues. At the "renewal" level, the user reevaluates the innovation to seek major ways it can be modified to increase its impact, as well as seeking additional alternatives and new goals.

There is also the problem that a label used to describe a change does not necessarily mean the same thing to different people. As noted in our earlier reference to Gallagher (1967), a particular innovation may take several different forms, even in the same school building. Charters and Jones (1974) commented on the difficulty of measuring the impact of experimental programs in education because the independent, manipulable variable (i.e., the innovative program itself) tends to vary so much in quality and configuration from site to site. What is meant by the term "team teaching"? What is meant by a "modified block schedule"? What is meant by "teaching for critical thinking"? Although each of these terms and phrases will bring a number of common concepts to mind, every experienced educator knows that there can be great diversity in the way in which any of these innovations are implemented.

How can one measure the effect of any planned change when the label used to describe it means different things to different people? The CBAM dimension of Innovation Configurations is addressed to this need to understand the operational definition of an innovation.

In order to understand the change process there is a need to identify the configurations that an innovation may take. Hall and Hord (p. 124) propose that this identification process follow eight steps:

STEP 1: Ask the developer of the innovation to identify the innovation components; also ask the facilitator(s) to identify the innovation components.

STEP 2: Develop the first draft of a checklist.

STEP 3: Interview and observe a small number of users.

STEP 4: Adjust the checklist.

STEP 5: Interview and observe a larger number of users.

STEP 6: Construct a semifinal checklist; check with the innovation expert(s) and make final revisions.

STEP 7: Collect data and analyze to identify dominant configurations.

STEP 8: Design in-service based on teacher practice; use data in evaluation analysis.

Thus the CBAM Model supplies the principal with a relatively sophisticated, yet usable, model to analyze the complex process of change in the school. By focusing on the three dimensions as they interact and develop over time, the principal and other leaders in the school can significantly increase their understanding of the change process and the likelihood that their plans for change will have the impact they desire.

## CONTEXT AND COLLABORATION: CONNECTING WITH THE ENVIRONMENT

Hall and Hord (1987) also emphasize the importance of the context in which the school operates for understanding the change process. The organizational context of each school is unique, and it is impossible to make formal prescriptions for implementing change that can be applied without modification to schools generally. What Hall and Hord have contributed with their three-dimensional CBAM model is to provide some tools for understanding how the complex interrelationships within the school and those that link the school with its community and other agencies can be used to diagnose potential for change in the school and plot a course of action to accomplish it.

Seymour Sarason (1971, 1982) has also explored the significance of a school's context in planning and implementing change in considerable depth. He gives particular emphasis to the "culture" of the school and describes how the values and regularities that are part of this culture often inhibit change and make it difficult for the school to relate to outside agencies in a mutually productive way. He emphasizes the importance of understanding the organizational and cultural context in planning change and describes in some detail cases where change has been effective and where it has been ineffective. He also gives considerable attention (particularly in the 1971 version of his book) to the role of the principal in the change process.

The school that would change what it is doing to better serve both its students and the larger society is faced with a dilemma. By relying strictly on its own resources, it often fails to recognize the need for change or, if a need for change is sensed, to usefully specify the nature of a change that is needed. Part of the school's problem in this regard is that it takes its own operation so much for granted that it is difficult to perceive where difficulties really lie or to envision suitable alternatives. It is often difficult to generate ideas that will truly change "the ways we've always done things." As noted by many observers, the fish is not aware of the water in which it swims.

On the other hand, if assistance in bringing about change is sought from an outside agency, such as a university, the problems of the school as well as their remedies are often envisioned primarily in terms of the culture, agenda, and the expertise of that agency. Sarason (1982) has highlighted some of the problems that are likely to result when universities and schools try to work together. The school's problems are likely to be seen in light of what the university feels it does well, rather than in terms of what the school needs. The university, in working with the school, is likely to take on a professorial role and give knowledge and direction to the school. The school, with its own culture and restrictions, often cannot respond satisfactorily to the university's direction, and its unresponsiveness is seen as obstinacy or incompetence. Given the complexity of both the school structure and any significant change, there is much that needs to be learned by school and university. All parties in the change process must become learners. Yet the university's culture does not readily allow it to take on the role of learner. It is often not a much easier role for the school, which is also in the business of telling other people what they should know. Collaborative relationships are difficult to forge; they are more difficult to implement.

James Comer (1980) has provided an excellent extended case study of how one such collaborative effort between school and university was initiated and sustained and was ultimately highly successful. Comer's description of a collaborative intervention project between the Child Study Center of Yale University and the New Haven (Connecticut) schools provides considerable insight into the complexity of change, the impact of the context in which change takes place, and the requirements for successful school-university collaboration. Perhaps the greatest value of Comer's work to the principal who would envision change in his or her school is that it does not ignore the difficulties of the change process. Failures and program restarts, as well as successes, are faithfully described by Comer. Comer clearly demonstrates that only by providing an open climate that promotes valid two-way communication and the honest recognition of school problems can workable solutions be reached. He also clearly describes the postures that are required of both school and university personnel if productive collaboration is to take place.

Comer's case study also provides an excellent description of what Fullan (1993) calls a learning organization. Through Comer's multi-year description we see everyone learning: students, teachers, school administrators, university professors, etc. Fullan makes the point emphatically that it is not possible for the school to nurture learning in its students unless the school also nurtures learning in teachers, the principal, and other adults. Fullan joins Sergiovanni (1992) in calling for a new leadership for change in the school that infuses learning, moral purpose, and power in all members of the organization.

In short, the process for successfully initiating and implementing change in the school is essentially no different from what we have prescribed for the school's regular mode of operation. The lessons we learn from the writings of Comer (1980), Sarason (1982), and Fullan (1993) lead us back to Chapter 2 and the Model II pattern of professional interaction described by Argyris and Schön (1974, 1978). The free flow of valid information among all the school's stakeholders needs to be maximized. Each stakeholder must participate in the school organization through a series of free and informed choices. Every individual must see him or herself as an origin of solutions, as a significant power in the enterprise. In short, each individual must be empowered to speak and to act in support of the school's mission. What must be built into the process is an internal commitment on the part of every individual to the vision of the school, to the implementation of that vision, and to the monitoring of that implementation to ensure that it works.

## RESPONDING TO A NEGATIVE ENVIRONMENT: A SPECIAL CASE OF PLANNED CHANGE

Often the school is forced to change in response to external forces. The last years of the twentieth century have witnessed drastic changes imposed on schools by shrinking resources. Such pressures usually mean cutting back on personnel, and this means personal discomfort and suffering. This, in turn, can be traumatic for the entire school organization. When the humans in an organization are suffering, the mission of the organization is in jeopardy. The principal has a responsibility both to all the school's stakeholders and to the fulfillment of the school's mission. (See Fig. 6.6.)

But restructuring, even when caused by negative sources, provides opportunities for growth. One of the authors was faced with just such a problem when severe loss of financial resources forced her school district to cut back on many fronts.

She found the work of Bridges (1991) very useful as she prepared her campus for dealing with restructuring.

According to Bridges, it is very important for the principal to provide information on the grief process as it applies to change. When staff members are faced with major changes, they need to realize that they will experience various known stages of grief: anger, bargaining, anxiety, sadness, disorientation, and depression. Further, the principal also needs to take certain other steps:

- Help people in compensating for losses;
- Give people valid information, and do it again and again;
- Define what is over and what isn't;
- Mark the endings of things that are over;
- Treat the past with respect, let people take a piece of the old with them;
- Show how endings ensure continuity with what really matters.

The major restructuring that was forced on the school district had a heavy and direct impact on the elementary school of which the author was principal. Title I restructuring created a $100,000 cut in her campus budget. This led to an elimination of three personnel units, major adjustments in the reading and mathematics program, and a rewriting of the Campus Improvement Plan. In addition, the restructuring provided an Early Out Incentive Program for staff who met certain eligibility criteria for retirement. On her campus, with the Early Out Incentive Program and other personnel moves, there was the potential for a change of 10 people out of a staff of 60. In order to help the people on the staff have an opportunity to deal with this change, she planned a final faculty/staff meeting.

A breakfast meeting was held with all faculty and staff members. During the meeting the principal reiterated what she believed they were losing and what they were not losing. She had the entire staff respond individually to two questions:

What do you think about all the changes?

How do you feel about them?

This gave everyone the opportunity to do several important things:

♦ Publicly acknowledge the changes, both those that were imminent and those that were pending.

♦ Publicly acknowledge and demonstrate respect for the contributions of individual staff members.

♦ Articulate their thoughts and feelings regarding all the changes.

The session was filled with laughter and tears and proved to be an excellent way to empower everyone to say "Good-bye" to the past, thereby making it possible to say "Hello" to the future.

In order to facilitate the massive changes at the district level, a meeting was planned for all the district principals, top central office staff, and all other individuals whose jobs were being restructured. This meeting was planned around lunch, decorated for a "New Year's Celebration, "and organized to create a party atmosphere. Live entertainment was furnished, and autograph ribbons ("autographs of the rich and famous") were provided for everyone to sign. A timeline, "Acknowledging the Past and Moving into the Future," was created. The timeline included a number of significant dates, detailing historical events in the district, and invited everyone to add to it. The program consisted of recognizing all of the retirees and then having toasts (using apple cider and champagne glasses) made by a variety of people. A final toast was made to the new year of change. This activity provided unique closure to a very difficult year and made it possible for participants to leave with positive feelings about themselves and about each other.

Restructuring, even though it has a very negative side, also provides a school with new opportunities. First and foremost it can refocus the attention of the principal, the retained staff, and other stakeholders on the mission of the school. Certain key questions are raised:

What can we do now?

What can't we do?

Can we do things more effectively and efficiently than we have in the past? If so, how?

What changes should we make in the way we do things? How will we monitor these changes?

Such questions can enhance ownership and collaboration, even in a time of human disappointment and suffering. Principal, faculty, staff, and other school stakeholders must embrace the attitude that, in spite of all the negative things that have happened, their primary duty is still to the students. They must embrace the belief that by planning and working together collaboratively they can effectively serve the future of those students.

## ACTION FOLLOW-UP

- ◆ Describe an innovation that you would like to initiate and implement in your school. Complete a Change Potential Analysis Chart (CPAC) to analyze how the proposed innovation would affect the various stakeholders. Share your analysis with other persons who will be involved in implementing the innovation.

- ◆ Use the Concerns Based Adoption Model (CBAM) of Hall and Hord, or some other model, to prepare for the implementation of an innovation in your school. Share this analysis and preparation with other persons who will be involved in implementing the innovation.

- ◆ Working together with other school stakeholders, use your CPAC and CBAM analyses to develop a plan for initiating, implementing, and monitoring an innovation in your school.

# 7

# ORGANIZING FOR EXCELLENCE

Principals often feel somewhat overwhelmed by the multi-dimensional complexity of their role. As we have documented throughout the book, feelings of inadequacy and frustration are not unfounded. The job is a tough one that pulls its incumbents in many directions, and we might question whether principals who never feel intimidated a little by the scope of responsibilities really have good touch with the realities of their jobs or the true nature of the school's mission. Yet we have innumerable examples of principals who, in seemingly impossible situations, have turned schools around and, in the worst of situations, have turned their schools into outstanding learning organizations. We believe that one of the skills that makes this possible is the complex skill of organizational oversight that we have addressed in this book.

Organizational oversight begins with an understanding of the school's organization. Any principal, whether new in the school or many years on the job, might begin the task of getting the school on track through an informal, yet comprehensive, organizational oversight audit. This audit begins by the principal asking him or herself a series of questions about the status of the school organization and the processes that occur in it. The questions we would propose are not difficult, but they do require complete honesty on the part of the principal and a willingness to face and admit some rather uncomfortable truths about the organization. If this honesty and willingness are not present, the proposed audit is a complete waste of time. While these qualities will not by themselves solve the principal's organizational problems, they will permit the principal to establish a framework that will allow the planning of specific changes and the development of organizational remedies.

While we suggest that the audit process begin with the principal him or herself, we do not recommend that it end there. After reviewing the audit questions alone, we suggest that the principal identify two or more trusted colleagues (including, if possible, at least one who is likely to see things differently from the way the principal sees them) to also respond to the audit questions. Their separate audits can be compared with the principal's and furnish the basis for dialogue and discussion that focuses on their separate responses. The principal and his/her colleagues (perhaps team members) should use this audit exercise as a learning experience in which they can each expand their own horizons and collectively build a richer understanding of the school organization and what needs to be done to strengthen it.

We would propose these questions for this informal audit process:

- ◆ Do the various stakeholders of the school genuinely value the maximization of valid information?
  Is this answer different for different groups of stakeholders?
  If you're not certain about the answers to this question, how can you find the answers out?
- ◆ Does communication flow effectively throughout the school and among its various stakeholders?
  Is this communication multidirectional?
  Are there blockages in communication? Where are they?
  Is there communication overload? Should alternative channels be used? Should additional channels be created?
  Should ineffective channels be eliminated?
- ◆ Have you, your leadership team members, and other stakeholders learned to dialogue and not just discuss?
  How can you learn to dialogue? What steps do you need to take to facilitate this learning?

- Does the school have a strategic planning process in place?

  Does the strategic plan effectively use a mixed scanning process?

  Are different alternatives genuinely considered?

  Is the plan based on input from all the school's stakeholders?

  Does the strategic plan use *focused trial and error* to progressively improve its limited knowledge?

  Is there an attitude of *tentativeness* that produces corrections and modifications in practice?

  Are *procrastination, decision staggering,* and *fractionalizing* used in the strategic planning process?

  Are *reversible* decisions made? Have *irreversible* decisions been made?

  What tools have been adopted to support the strategic planning process?

- Are annual planning documents (the master calendar, the class schedule, and the campus plan) coordinated with strategic planning?

  Are these annual planning documents appropriately written for their intended audiences?

  Are annual planning documents appropriately used by teachers, students, and parents?

  What handbooks and other documents are available to inform teachers, students, and parents about the school program and its policies? Are they appropriately used by these groups? What gaps do they leave? What additional topics might be included in handbooks or similar documents?

- Do things often feel out of control at the school?

  Do you often miss deadlines for important work?

  Do you often miss appointments?

  Do you take time to answer phone calls (or otherwise ensure that they are answered)?

  Do you often find yourself attending to matters (responding to phone calls, meeting with salespeople, etc.) that could be better handled (or more efficiently handled) by someone else on your staff?

Do you often feel overwhelmed by the number of items to which you must respond?

Do you have time for yourself, to be with your family, and to participate in other important nonschool activities?

Are there often many people in your office (students, teachers, parents, etc.) waiting to see you?

Do you have time for strategic planning?

Do you have time to work with teachers on instructional mat-ters?

Do you have time to help teachers with their professional development?

♦ What innovations have been introduced into your school in recent years? What is their status now?

What changes do you plan to implement? To what extent have your plans recognized the complexity of change and the readiness of various stakeholders for change?

What are the chief obstacles to innovation and planned change in your school?

There are no answers to these questions that are right or wrong for every case. The right answers are those that accurately reflect what is happening in the school. If answers are honestly sought to these questions, they can give the principal a fairly comprehensive picture of how effectively organizational oversight is operating in the school. This, in turn, gives the principal the basis for improving his/her organizational skills and using them to facilitate the implementation of the school's vision. This has been the major theme of this book.

# REFERENCES

Argyris, C. & Schön, D.A. (1974). *Theory in Practice: Increasing Professional Effectiveness.* San Francisco: Jossey-Bass.

Argyris, C. & Schön, D.A. (1978). *Organizational learning: A theory of action perspective.* Reading, MA: Addison-Wesley.

Bridges, W. (1991). *Managing Transitions, Making the Most of Change.* Reading, MA: Addison-Wesley.

Charters, W.W. & Jones J.E. (1974). *On Neglect of the Independent Variable.* Project MITT Occasional Paper. Eugene, OR: Center for Educational Policy and Management, University of Oregon.

Comer, J.P. (1980). *School Power: Implications of an Intervention Project.* New York: The Free Press.

Cunningham, W.G. (1982). *Systematic Planning for Educational Change.* Palo Alto, CA: Mayfield Publishing Company.

Cyert, R.M. & March J.G. (1992). *A Behavioral Theory of the Firm.* Cambridge, MA: Blackwell Publishers.

Downey, L. (1960). *The Task of Public Education.* Chicago: The University of Chicago Press.

Eichholz, G. & Rogers, E.M. (1964). Resistance to the Adoption of Audio-Visual Aids by Elementary School Teachers: Contrasts and Similarities to Agricultural Innovation. In M.B. Miles, *Innovation in Education.* New York: Teachers College, Columbia University.

Erlandson, D.A. (1972). The Principal: Power or Pawn? *NASSP Bulletin, 56* (368), 1–10.

Erlandson, D.A. (1976). *Strengthening School Leadership.* Danville, IL: The Interstate Printers & Publishers, Inc.

Erlandson, D.A. (1980). An Organizing Strategy for Managing Change in the School. *NASSP Bulletin, 64* (435), 1–8.

Etzioni, A. (1967). Mixed Scanning: A Third Approach to Decision Making. *Public Administration Review, 27* 385–392.

Etzioni, A. (1986). Mixed Scanning Revisited. *Public Administration Review, 46,* 8–14.

Etzioni, A. (1989). Humble Decision Making. *Harvard Business Review, 67* (4), 122–126.

Fullan, M. (1993). *Change Forces: Probing the Depths of Educational Reform* London: The Falmer Press.

Gallagher, J.J. (1967). Teacher Variation in Concept Presentation in BSCS Curriculum Programs. *BSCS Newsletter, 30*, 8–19.

Hall, G.E. & Hord, S.M. (1987). *Change in Schools: Facilitating the Process*. Albany, NY: State University of New York Press.

Hoy, W.K. & Tarter, C.J. (1995). *Administrators Solving the Problems of Practice*. Boston: Allyn and Bacon.

Leithwood, K. (1993). Contributions of Transformational Leadership to School Restructuring. An invited address to the 1993 Convention of the University Council for Educational Administration, Houston, Texas.

Likert, R. (1961). *New Patterns of Management*. New York: McGraw-Hill Book Company, Inc.

Likert, R. (1967). *The Human Organization: Its Management and Value*. New York: McGraw-Hill Book Company, Inc.

Lightfoot, S.L. (1983). *The Good High School*. New York: Basic Books, Inc.

Lippitt, G.L. (1973). *Visualizing Change: Model Building and the Change Process*. Fairfax, VA: NTL Learning Resource Corporation, Inc.

McCalla, S.A. (1987). The Relationship Between the Communication Structure of a High School and Faculty Perceptions of School Climate. (Unpublished Doctoral Dissertation, Texas A&M University.)

Mayhew, K.C. & Edwards, A.C. (1936). *The Dewey School*. New York: D. Appleton-Century Company, Incorporated.

Sarason, S.B. (1971, 1982). *The Culture of the School and the Problem of Change*. Boston: Allyn and Bacon, Inc.

Senge, P. (1990). *The Fifth Discipline: The Art and Practice of the Learning Organization*. New York: Doubleday Company.

Sergiovanni, T. J. (1992). *Moral Leadership: Getting to the Heart of School Improvement*. San Francisco: Jossey-Bass Publishers.

Stufflebeam, D.L., Foley, W.J., Gephart, W.J., Guba, E.J., Hammond, R.L., Merriman, H.O., and Provus, M.M. (1971). *Educational Evaluation and Decision Making*. Itasca, IL: Peacock Publishers.

Thomson, Scott D., Editor (1993). *Principals for Our Changing Schools: The Knowledge and Skill Base*. Fairfax, VA: National Policy Board for Educational Administration.